ThaDoggfather

the times, trials, and hardcore truths

Snoop Dogg

with
Davin Seay

ThaDoggfather

of snoop dogg

william morrow and company, inc. | new york

Library of Congress Cataloging-in-Publication Data

Snoop Dogg (Musician)
    Tha Doggfather: the times, trials, and hardcore truths of Snoop Dogg/Snoop Dogg,
with Davin Seay.
    p. cm.
    ISBN 0-688-17158-3
    1. Snoop Dogg (Musician) 2. Rap musicians—United States—Biography. I.
Title. II. Seay, Davin.

ML420.S6735A3 1999
782.421649'092—dc21
[B]

782.421649
Sn 54d

99-046608

Printed in the United States of America

First Edition

1 2 3 4 5 6 7 8 9 10

BOOK DESIGN BY DEBBIE GLASSERMAN

www.williammorrow.com

to my grandfather, Jeremiah Tate (R.I.P.); this one's for you.

—snoop dogg

to my homeboy hector.

—davin seay

acknowledgments

My family—my teachers, the homies, DPG, LPC; No Limit Records; my momz, Beverly, and my pops, Vernell; my wife, Shanté, and three kids, Cordé, Cordell, and Cori; my grandmother, Dorothy; my auntie Gail; my brothers Jerry and Bing; my cousin Joe Cool; my uncle June Bug; and the Broadus family, Varnado family, and Tate family.

A special thank you to William Clark, Hadley Murrell, Jonathan Pillot, Donald Randall, Ali Ryan, Steve Sabo, Davin Seay, Pat Shannahan, and Jimmy Vines: "For all your hard work in making this book happen."
—snoop dogg

William Clark for exemplary agenting, Jimmy Vines for solid support, and Paul Bresnick for extreme editorial aplomb. And Snoop Dogg for letting me tell this story.
—davin seay

ThaDoggfather

the

dog-
father

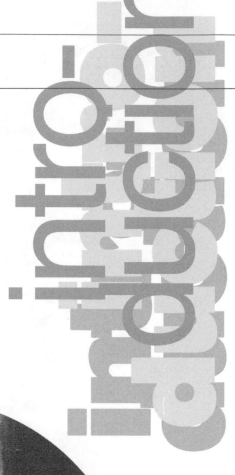

intro-
duction

introduction

o increase the peace.

To spread the music.

To elevate and educate.

If you don't get past another line in this book, go back and read those words again. Then read them one more time.

You might never hear another thing about me, who I am and where I'm coming from. But if you remember those words you'll know all you need to about Snoop Dogg. Straight from the source.

Because you've probably already heard what everybody else has to say on the subject:

Crack cocaine dealer. Ex-con. Accused murderer.

Rap star. Family man. Loyal son of Long Beach, California.

But none of that shit matters. The good or the bad. It's all just pictures on the late news. Headlines in a morning paper. Images in a mirror you're only holding up to yourself. What matters is increasing the peace. Spreading the music. Elevating and educating.

That's my mission. Because no matter who you think I am, or who you want me to be, when it all comes down, I only answer to one description:

I'm a child of God. Doing God's work.

I've been put on this scene for a reason. I've got a goal to accomplish.

And every time a black man lays down a piece, or a pipe; every time he holds back his hand from slapping his woman and hangs onto his pride by being a father to his kids; every time one of my brothers or sisters takes a stand for what's righteous and real . . . I'm one step closer to accomplishing that goal. Their history is my history. Their hopes are my hopes. See, when it's all said and done, we all come from the same 'hood.

As you maybe can tell already, I'm not really down with that celebrity shit. God gave me talent and ability and ambition and then put me to the test to prove I was worthy. It's the standard game He runs on everyone. The only reason I'm up here and you're down there—if that's the way you really want to see it—is because He had something else in mind for the two of us. It's this way today. Tomorrow could be something totally different.

Maybe you envy me. Maybe you're jealous of all the stuff you think I got that you don't. Maybe you wish you could be just like me, working my game and busting my moves.

But it's not like that. Being where I am, being *who* I am, was never about what I could get. But it was always about what I could give. Understand: I've got responsibilities. And not just to my family or my record company or even all my homies back in the L.B.C., looking for one of their own to make it out and make them proud. I've got a responsibility to God. He put me here. He'll take me down in a heartbeat the minute I start tripping on myself and how great I must be because of all the people telling me all the time.

That's why I've got to stay real, to remember where I came from and where I'm going. See, I didn't get sent out on this mission with nothing to cover my ass in a crossfire. A powerful weapon has been put at my disposal.

The truth.

In every rap I ever recorded, in the mad flow of every street-corner freestyle I ever represented, there was only one thing I wanted to get across: the way that it is. Not the way I might want it to be. Not the way I think *you* might want it to be. But the way it *really* is, on the streets of the 'hoods of America, where life is lived out one day at a time, up against it, with no guarantees.

I tried to keep it real, never to sell the truth, but always to tell the truth. And if there's one reason why you know the name Snoop Dogg and I don't know yours, it's because telling the truth has given me the props I need to carry out God's purpose and plan.

And I'm not about to stop now. Brothers ask me why I felt it was necessary to write a book, my autobiography, and put down in black and white what I usually put down in rhyme and rhythm.

The answer is simple. My raps describe what it's like to be a young black man in America today. This book describes how, for one young black American, it got to be that way. My music is the end. My life is the means. And there couldn't be one without the other.

Brothers talk to me about "telling my side of the story" and "setting the record straight." But I've got no time for that shit. A man that's got to defend himself has already lost his self-respect. Whoever you already think I am, where I come from, and what I'm trying to do, is strictly your point of view. I'll leave you to deal with your own reality and let my music and my life speak for themselves. If you want to know how it really is, and how it got that way, you can read my book. But if you think you already got me figured out, you're just wasting your time. You can walk away now. It's not up to me tó justify gangsta rap, ghetto life, or gang warfare. I'm not interested in making a case for my innocence when it comes to a certain well-publicized case of murder in the first. I don't have to convince you, or anybody else, that Snoop Dogg is straight up. This book isn't ever going to be about pleading my case in the court of public opinion. Fuck that shit.

This book is not a defense. It's a description. I want people to take the time, with an open mind, to look behind what they've been told about me and the world I come from, and hear the truth. The truth will set you free, is how one brother said it a long time ago, and I learned something about being free a long time ago, too. It comes with a price. I'm just passing that along, for whatever you think it's worth.

I paid the price to get myself free, from drugs and violence, from incarceration and intoxication, and from fear and death of every description. I paid the price so that maybe you don't have to, so that maybe when you read this book you can take a lesson from me, avoid my mistakes, and share my success. Like I said, I'm about elevating and educating. What I can teach comes straight out of my life. What you can learn goes straight into yours. We're here to help each other. God taught me that.

Of course, I can't promise anything. You may put down this book still wondering how a nigger named Snoop Dogg got all the breaks. Or you may never pick it up in the first place, convinced up front that a nigger named Snoop Dogg couldn't possibly tell you anything you need to know.

And the truth is, there was a time when I might have agreed with you. If a brother comes from where I do, where all his life he might only ever see people just like him—the same color, wearing the same clothes, driving the same cars, and eating the same food—it'd be hard to blame that brother for believing that anyone who didn't dress, drive, or dine like him wouldn't understand the first thing about his life. Hell, you live in the ghetto long enough, you'll be talking a *language* most people on the outside don't understand. And one of the things I've tried to do in this book is to put the words down in a way that most of the peeps can pick up on, while still staying true to myself.

But the fact is, the more I get out and take a look around, the more other brothers and sisters seem to have in common with the homies on my own turf. I've been all around America, across Europe and way up into Scandinavia, and if anyone ever tells you that hardcore hip-hop music is by blacks, for blacks, about blacks, you tell him to come by one of my concerts in Oslo or Copenhagen or Stockholm, where as far as you can see is an ocean of pale faces, blue eyes, and blond hair, and every one of them jamming hard and heavy like they were partying at a Compton club on a Saturday night.

So, if you're thinking I've got nothing to say to you, just ask those Swedes: truth comes in many disguises, even a skinny nigger with braids from the east side of Long Beach, California.

Looking out at those happy white people, bumping to the beat, flashing signs and singing along to my words, I'd have to ask myself, What are they getting out of all this? How is it that they can relate to hip-hop as strong as anybody that's as black as I am? What's the connection?

And the answer comes back around to being real. It doesn't matter what color you are—anything that's got the ring of truth, you got to deal with one way or the other. And whether you love it, hate it, or try to run away from it doesn't really matter. The truth never changes. It's us that have to accommodate.

So I just tell the truth and let the rest of you motherfuckers sort it out for yourselves. And the truth is simple, not some complicated philosophy or metaphysical concept. The truth I tell comes from the streets, where every day is a matter of life and death, where what matters is family loyalty and honor in the 'hood and a code of survival that can't be betrayed.

People all around the world understand that because it's straight up, black and white and no bullshit. Like the Wild West, it's part of the American Dream. You stake out your turf and you defend it with your life. You take the law into your own hands because, sure as hell, no cavalry's going to come riding over the hill just in time to save your ass. You've got to take a stand to protect what's yours. You cut your deals and pick your homies and wear your colors because you've got to— there's no middle ground, no place to hide, no way to escape the consequences of the choices you make. It's dog eat dog, kill or be killed, do unto others before they do unto you.

So whether you call the game Cops and Robbers, Cowboys and Indians, or Crips and Bloods, it comes down to the same thing: life lived out on the extreme edge. And where you're at with that depends on what your own life looks like on the inside.

Maybe you're holding down a nine-to-five, paying out on a second mortgage, with child support, alimony, car payments . . . all that shit. Maybe your life was locked down from jump, set to unroll all by itself, right on schedule from cradle to grave. Maybe it was all safe and secure and settled from the minute you popped out and they put your name on a plastic bracelet around your wrist.

And maybe that shit is getting old. You might look around and ask yourself, "Is this all there is?" and then you hear one of my songs on the radio or catch a video on MTV and suddenly it all starts looking a whole lot larger than life—your sorry life, anyway. In Snoop Dogg's world, the bad guys are badder, the good guys are gooder, the scrilla is fatter, and the women are finer than you've ever seen. But, most of all, in my world you can read the rules. You know who your friends are.

You can spot your enemies a mile away. Life is more precious because death can be waiting around any corner, at any time.

But that's only part of it. Just like that cowboy movie in your mind, you see the stranger ride into town, the young gun with the fastest rap in the West, who takes on the baddest motherfucker in the territory and rides off into the sunset, a legend in his own time. And it looks good to you, the way life should be.

So you buy my records and put my poster up on your wall and talk like me and walk like me and dress like me and even if you don't, you still wish you could. There's a reason hip-hop music outsells rock & roll two to one. Because little white kids living in gated communities across this country want to be down with the brothers in the 'hood. We *represent* something to them—a freedom their mama and daddy can't ever buy.

But remember what I said about being free? One way or the other, you've got to pay the price.

Check it out: if you think I've come to tell you that that whole cowboys-in-the-ghetto movie dream of yours is just so much media bullshit they try to sell you like cornflakes or Preparation H, you're in the wrong book.

Damn straight, life in the ghetto is like the Wild West.

Damn straight, homies live by the code of frontier justice.

Damn straight, a rapper can make his name if he's got what it takes.

I'd be lying if I told you anything else, and I already told you—I don't lie.

But a half-truth is no better than a lie. So, before you're done making a myth out of my life, listen up to the other half of the story.

Bullets make you bleed.

Drugs kill your soul.

All the cheddar and fine bitches in the world won't make you any less dead than all the brothers and sisters I've known and loved whose faces I'll never see again.

Tupac ain't coming back. Neither is Biggie. Neither are a thousand other niggers in 'hoods just like yours and mine who died for reasons I couldn't begin to explain.

That's the other half of the story. That's the part I need this book to tell. Otherwise, I wouldn't be living up to my responsibility, the mission God sent me on. I'm not about telling you how to live your life, warning you about the wages of sin, or handing out advice you didn't ask for. But there's a reason I've been put in this place. That doesn't make me so special. It doesn't put me up above you. We all got a reason we're here, a mission to accomplish and a destiny to fulfill. Maybe the only difference between you and me is that I know my reason.

To tell the truth.

The whole truth.

And nothing but.

The truth is, there's nothing about my life I would change. I take the good with the bad, and even though there's some shit that went down that I wish I could say hadn't, I know God's got a reason for everything He does.

He's even got a reason for this book.

To increase the peace.

To spread the music.

To elevate and educate.

Which brings me back to where I started. And I guess if you've read this far, it means you're going to hang with my story for a while.

It starts out like this . . .

chapter one

Ebony, ivory, and me—working out a riff at age seven.

chapter one

You'll be driving down the freeway, the 405 from L.A., through O.C., on down to San Diego. Maybe you're heading to Disneyland with a carful of kids. Or maybe you and your homies are out to have some kind of illegal fun, 'cross the border in Tijuana.

You get down past LAX, moving on through Torrance and over by the oil refinery right off the side of the road in Commerce, with flames shooting right out the motherfucking smokestacks, like the devil smoking chronic. Then you hit the straightaway coming up on Signal Hill and maybe you get a look at the Queen Mary in the harbor off in the distance, but you don't think to stop. You'll just be moving through, getting past nowhere on your way to somewhere else.

But if you took the time to turn off one of those exits and drop down through all those side streets of one-family homes and mom-and-pop liquor stores and schoolyard hoops, down around Lewis Avenue or Corinth Street or on out Twentieth right through the east side of Long Beach, you'd be crossing the border, the demilitarized no-man's-land, into *my* world.

Take a look around—there's no place like it on the planet, and even though it might seem like any other urban battle zone in any other ghetto 'hood from here to D.C., this is *my* 'hood and no one could be prouder of where they call home than I am of Long Beach, California.

I expect most people feel that way about the place they come from, whether you were born in a city or a small town, a castle or a shack. When you're a kid that's your world, and everything you know, from horizon to horizon, is situated right there. And when people think of the ghettos of Los Angeles, they most likely fix on the famous ones—Watts or Compton—where brothers burn shit down and got attitude. But, for me, those places are just names on a map, exit ramps *I* drive past to get where *I'm* going. For me, Long Beach'll always be the one place where I know I can always come back, no matter how far off I've gone or how long I've been away.

Long Beach may not be much to look at, at least not the east side, which was my turf growing up. Neighbors along the block tried to keep their front lawns mowed and their fences painted, store owners knew the names of their regular customers, and you could always get into a pickup game down in the schoolyard at Roosevelt or Lafayette or Cleveland Elementary. But, aside from that, you probably wouldn't give it another thought. It was like any other town at the edge of a big city, where whites moved on and left the streets to the blacks. But Long Beach was my home, my 'hood. I loved it, and I always will.

That might seem strange, speaking about the ghetto like that. Most of the time, you hear about people trying to get *away* from places like the east side of Long Beach, moving out and up to a more respectable address and leaving their roots behind. And, sure enough, these days, I don't live in Long Beach myself. Part of that has got to do with the 'hood not being the way it used to be, the way I remember it growing up. Part of it has to do with *me* changing and growing and moving on. But I never thought of my hometown as a place I had to escape from. I'm part of it, and it's part of me . . . the best part, the part I'm proudest of.

The family I came up in, the homies I ran with, the secrets I kept, and the lessons I learned: those are the things that make a man who he is, and the man I am found his way on the streets of Long Beach.

People think living in the ghetto is all about misery—about rats and roaches, crime and poverty. And we had all that, but we never cried about our place and felt sorry for each other. We never whined or complained or looked at what someone else had and wanted to take it away. We were proud of where we lived, and we took all, the good and bad, together, because that's the way it came to us. You deal with what you got and in Long Beach, California, what you've got is *identity*—a place where you belong and people you belong to.

That's how I remember it, anyway. And, if the 'hood didn't exactly stay the same as it was back in the day, then it's up to the youngbloods out there now to make it into the place *they* want it to be. A 'hood is only as good as the friends and neighbors who call it home. And I was blessed to be born in Long Beach.

That event came to pass at the Los Altos Hospital on October 20, 1971. I was the second of three boys born to Beverly Broadus, who herself had come out to California years before looking for a life a little better than the one she knew as a sharecropper's daughter in McComb, Mississippi.

It was back in McComb that my mama first met my daddy, Vernall Varnado, himself a son of the Deep South who was also looking for a way out. I still have a lot of family down that way, both my grandmothers and a few aunts and uncles, but growing up, McComb, Mississippi, might as well have been on the dark side of the moon. Like I said, my world ended at Long Beach city limits.

I *do* remember a trip we took out that way when I was a few years old, though. The recollections are dim, but a picture of all that flat farmland laid out as far as the eye could see is still fresh in my mind.

My memories of my daddy are a lot less fresh. The truth is, he wasn't around too much, and in that I guess I wasn't much different from a whole lot of other kids growing up in single-parent homes in ghettos across the country. I've come to believe that fatherless families are the curse of American blacks, and my own history is the main reason I've made a solid promise to my own family that I'll always be there for them.

My mama and daddy were together for a few years before my older brother, Jerry, was born, just after Vernall left for Vietnam, when he was nineteen years old. I was born a year after he got off active duty, but by the time I was old enough to walk he'd pretty much dropped out of my life for good.

I wish I could say I understood what made him walk away from his responsibilities like that, leaving behind a wife and two young children, but the truth is, I don't. Maybe one day I'll find a way to forgive and forget, but right now that's just not happening. There's no way he could explain to me what was up with him not being there, just like there's no way I could explain to him what it was like to grow up without a man in the house and the discipline and direction that comes with that.

But I guess my daddy *did* pass on one thing to me—a love for music. Even after he'd split, landing a job as a mail carrier and working a route in Detroit for ten years, I'd once in a while hear back about his musical ventures, singing gospel with some of my long-lost uncles in the Sensational Varnado Brothers and even putting out a couple of records. And I read every once in a while that it was Daddy who nicknamed me Snoop when I was a baby because I was supposed to resemble Snoopy, the dog in the *Peanuts* comic strip.

Personally, I doubt that that story is true, mostly because my daddy wasn't around enough when I was a baby to know *what* I looked like. But I really couldn't tell you for sure how I came by the name Snoop. It's not like my mama ever sat me down and told me what it was all about. Like anybody else, you just get a nickname and it sticks, long after everyone's forgotten why exactly they called you that in the first place. It's even happened with my own sons, Cordé and Cordell. I call Cordé "Spanky" because he reminds me of the youngster in *The Little Rascals*. And I call Cordell, the younger one, "Little Snoop," just because he reminds me of me. When they grow up they might ask me how they got those names, and if I remember I'll tell them. If not, they can make up their own story. It might be a better one, anyway.

For the record, the name on my birth certificate was Cordazar, which might be another reason I got tagged as Snoop right out of the cradle. Coming up, though, I mostly answered to Calvin, which was easier than Cordazar for sure, but not quite as dope as Snoop.

You might think my identity would get a little mixed up with all those different names, but from jump I never had any doubt about who exactly I was. I'll put it as simply as I can: I was my mama's baby. As much as my daddy was nowhere to be seen in those first years, it was just that much that my mama took up the slack.

The earliest memories I have are of my mama's loving me, holding me close, kissing my face and stroking my head and making me feel safe and secure and special in a way that only your mama can. Because of her, and her alone, there was never a time that I went without, never a minute when I didn't believe that I could do anything I put my heart and mind to, never a doubt that I had what it took to make something of myself. She gave me confidence and the feeling that I was worth something and, as much as you need food on the table and clothes on your back, a youngster needs to hear such things. When you're little and weak and don't know the rules of the game, you got to have a champion, someone who will look out for you, protect your ass, and make sure you got what you need to get what you want. You can fill a young child up with anything, make him a devil or an angel just by what you tell him about himself, and what my mama told me, every day of my life, was that she had faith in me, all the way.

She also had faith in God, a strong trust that never wavered and a belief that everything that happened to her and to her family was for a reason. She passed that on to me as well, and planted a seed that took deep root in my life.

It was a seed she made sure to water, every Sunday at the Trinity Baptist Church and every Tuesday night at a home Bible study. But my mama's religious training went way past going to church and following all the rules and regulations that make you a good Christian. She had a one-on-one connection to God, a way of talking with Him like He was in the same room or on the phone line, a free and easy flow, passing the time with her closest friend. She *knew* God heard her prayers, knew it like she knew her own face in the mirror, and she passed that confidence along to us, making sure we understood that, whatever we might be lacking in a father, God would make up for and then some.

The bottom line was that none of us kids ever felt underprivileged, disadvantaged, or inferior to anyone we might pass on the street, white or black. Mama loved us. God loved us. Nothing else mattered. And I'd carry that feeling of confidence around with me for the rest of my life, leaning on it hard those times when it seemed like the whole world was set up against me and I might never get free from the shit that was piling up. It was times like that when I knew that Mama had given me a gift more precious than gold or diamonds. She gave me a vision to see high things—and reach for them.

She also added to the taste for music that I'd gotten from my daddy's side. In fact, I'd have to say that Mama was one of my prime musical influences growing up. First off, there was the church. She herself was a member of the choir and, like her sisters, my aunts Dana and Dasmar, she had a sweet, pure voice that carried all the way back to the last pew, where all the Saturday night sinners were sitting nursing their hangovers and wincing every time she hit one of those clear, window-rattling notes. She eventually got me into the choir, too, and even though I was a little bit unsure about my voice, I truly loved being up in front of the people, styling in my Sunday best and singing for everything I was worth.

But it wasn't even so much the hymns and spirituals of Trinity Baptist that my mama gave me appreciation for, helping to wake me up to my own musical ambitions. As much as she loved singing about God, she gave herself just as much to singing along to the songs she heard on the radio. She was deep into old-school R&B, and she took me right along with her. Al Green, Teddy Pendergrass, the O'Jays, the Dramatics, the Stylistics—she dug them all and she made sure I was listening when one of her favorite hits came around.

And if the radio wasn't playing what she liked, she'd play it herself, from a collection of funky old eight-tracks she kept in the living room. She even made sure me and Jerry had a record player in our room, so, what with the radio in the kitchen and that beat-up tape player next to the TV, we had music in every room of the house, twenty-four seven.

I consider myself lucky to have grown up in the musical era I did. Some people will tell you that Motown was the golden age of soul music, but for me, nothing can touch the best sounds of the seventies. Those brothers had a sophistication and sense of style that built on everything that came before and pointed the way to a lot that was up and coming. You take Al Green, for instance. That nigger could sing! But it wasn't about shouting and testifying and trying to peel the paint off the wall. He had the *light* touch, like he was floating around inside the song, picking up a note here, dropping another there, giving you just a suggestion of the song and letting you fill in the spaces between the lines. Check out the arrangements of "Tired of Being Alone" or "I'm Still in Love With You" or "Let's Stay Together." Brother Al could say more by taking a deep breath and letting out it slow and sexy than a dozen other singers could by shouting at the top of their lungs. He was the master.

You might think a rapper is outside his game talking about singing and singers, but to me it's all just different ways of getting across the same thing. I don't claim that my raps have got anything to do with the way Al Green sings, except that I always try to say more with less, keep it cool, and don't get myself so excited you can't hear what I'm putting down. Come to think of it, maybe I *did* pick up something from the smooth style of the seventies superstars. But that's something you'll have to make up your own mind on.

I'll let you in on this, though: if it hadn't been for my mama and the way she kept music around us, like a movie soundtrack playing through our lives, I don't know if I'd be doing what I do today. Or at least not in exactly the same way. There was something about that combination of self-confidence and constant musical feedback that just naturally set me on this path. She not only made sure I felt like I had the ability to do whatever I wanted, she took the time to develop an interest in my talent that I might otherwise have never taken seriously. Sure, every ghetto kid wants to be either an athlete or an entertainer—those are mostly our role models to begin with. But how many of those youngsters are actually going to make it? I've been in this business long enough to know that talent is never enough. You've got to have determination, dedication, and a belief in yourself that no one can take away. Oh yeah, and a lot of just plain luck.

There was no way my mama could make me lucky. That just came because God wanted it. But she sure gave me all the rest. And some great sounds to grow up with, besides. I guess you could say that being born to her was the best luck of all. And for that, I'll be forever thankful.

chapter two

Snoop Dogg and Snoop Dad: Me and my pops, Vernall Varnado.

chapter two

he media's got an interest in making life in the ghetto out to be a living hell, with brothers shooting at each other all the time, crack on the playground, and pimps and whores on every street corner. That makes for a good headline, lots of drama and excitement and tragedy, even when the real story is just regular people trying their best to get by with what they've got, one day at a time.

It's true that life is harder today in places like the east side of Long Beach than they were when I was coming up. But it still isn't like what you hear on the news or see on all those cop shows. Mostly, trying to get by takes up all your time and energy, and even if the drugs and the violence and the poverty are for sure getting worse, brothers are still doing what they've got to do—going to work, raising their families, seeking a better future—without paying any mind to what the papers and the TV say is going on around them.

Most of the memories I have growing up probably aren't a whole lot different from the ones you've got. Kids are kids and they mostly are wanting and needing and hoping for the same kind of things no matter what side of the tracks they call home. Being poor was a fact of life in my family, but I couldn't tell you that I spent a lot of time sitting around thinking about all the disadvantages I was suffering under. About the worst it got was one Christmas when I was looking to get a

ColecoVision game like a homeboy down the street had and instead all I found under the tree was a pile of clothes and a ten-dollar bill. I was sure enough mad about it, but even then, I don't think it really hit me that I was any worse off than anyone else.

The fact is, as far as I could tell, I *wasn't.* Like I said, Long Beach was my whole world, and everyone in the 'hood was more or less at the same social and economic level. You're always hearing about democracy in America, and how everyone wants to be equal with everyone else. Straight up, there's no equalizer like being poor. It puts everybody in their place because no one can *afford* to have an attitude.

When I was coming up, I'd look around and everyone I saw was the same as me. East Long Beach was no integrated 'hood by any stretch of the imagination, no whites or Latinos on that turf, nothing but brothers. And what we saw on TV was like looking through a window into another world, where everything was shiny and new and about as real to us as a Saturday morning cartoon show.

In fact, our cartoons were *more* real to us than any of the shit we saw on prime time. As a youngster in the seventies, I consider myself lucky that there was a black consciousness finding its way into the mainstream in shows like *Fat Albert, Good Times,* and *What's Happening!!* The people in those programs looked like us, talked like us, had the same kind of problems as us, and worked them out like us. You couldn't ask for better role models. We'd see all those characters living in the ghetto and it made us feel cool to be there, too. If they could deal with it, so could we.

Same with the movies. *The Mack. Superfly. Foxy Brown. Black Caesar. Which Way Is Up? Uptown Saturday Night.* They all might have glorified a criminal mentality in the black community, but for us they were the bomb, good guys *we* could relate to and bad guys we could throw popcorn at. The soundtracks of those movies were like the soundtracks to our own lives. We'd be walking down the street with Marvin Gaye or Isaac Hayes playing in our heads like our own personal movie score, with us skinny little homies as the stars.

I guess, looking back, you could say that a lot of those hit black movies started putting up gangsters and drug dealers and pimps as outlaw heroes, but my take on that would be that there's no difference between what we were paying to see and the movie myths that whites lined up for. Maybe *The Godfather* had bigger stars and a megabudget, but the message wasn't all that different from *Superfly*. Maybe *Scarface* was about some Cuban crime lord, but it was the same drugs and violence that was getting everyone off, even while they were shaking their heads and shooting off their mouths about the lack of positive role models in the black community. Face it, there's nothing so tripped out about black America that you can't trace back to the culture at large. The only difference is, we're living it a lot closer to the edge. Whites might see a movie, get themselves a good look at all the sex and violence and the way the story shows how crime *does* pay, then they go home to their houses and turn on their personal security system and get a good night's sleep, knowing the forces of law and order are out patrolling their streets to protect their families and their property.

A black might see the same movie, then head on back to the ghetto, where the cops are looking for any excuse to drag his ass off to jail, where his minimum-wage McDonald's night-shift job can't even make the down payment on a Hyundai and half the brothers he knows are either in jail, on parole, or dead. The movie he just saw was like an informercial for a whole other way of life, one where you take what you want and keep what you get and never have to kiss anybody's ass in the process. He's been provided with a powerful temptation, and if the nigger succumbs to that temptation, you can blame him or you can blame the movie he just saw. Either way, if you keep lifting up those values and ideals, don't be surprised if, sooner or later, someone takes you at your word and grabs for what's dangling in front of them. People look around and wonder why the shit is spilling out of the ghetto onto the streets of their hometown, but you don't have to be a Ph.D. to figure that out—turn on your TV, tune in your radio, drop by the multiplex. We're all getting the same message. It's just that some of us have got more reason than others to believe in it.

If things are different today than when I was coming up, a child of the seventies, it's probably because we've had about thirty more years of the media trying to sell us on the lies and daydreams and fucking fantasies that they've been busy passing off as reality. I don't blame Hollywood for trying to turn gangsters into role models—any homeboy is responsible to himself for what he believes and who he chooses to follow—but I do know that what I'm about is telling the other side of the story through my music. Drugs kill. Guns kill. And when you're dead, you don't get up, wipe the fake blood off, and sit down for an Arby's roast beef sandwich. Someone's got to represent that reality, and if you're a part of the media game, you got that choice to make. It comes with the turf.

But naturally, movies and TV—good, bad, or indifferent—weren't the only influences I had growing up. When I was a couple of years old, my mama hooked up with a brother from New Jersey we called Big Bing. Like every other nickname you heard in the 'hood, mine included, the reason he got titled that way, I couldn't tell you. He was just Big Bing, and when he and mama had a baby together, my younger brother, it was just as natural to call *him* Little Bing.

I don't know whether Mama was being careful about getting married again after what happened with my daddy, or whether she just wanted to live her own life, her own way, but whatever the reason, she and Big Bing never did tie the knot. Regardless of that fact, though, I still considered him the closest thing to a real father that I had at the time, and some of my best memories as a youngster are the afternoons I spent over at his apartment watching sports on TV.

Big Bing was a good man, even if you counted the sad fact that he never did the right thing when it came to taking full responsibility for raising my little brother. In his own way, he tried to make things right in our family, treating the three of us like his own sons and taking the time to teach us the little things that only a man can show a boy.

His place was not too far from ours and there was a time when I spent nearly every weekend sitting on his couch while he explained to me the fine points of college football or professional hoops. He loved UCLA and the Lakers and he passed that love on to me, giving me that strong tie of hometown loyalty that is one of the things that makes sports such a powerful force for unity. Big Bing would spend hours talking out the game plans, handicapping the players, and cussing out the refs, but most important, he was letting me be a part of his world, and for that, I'll always carry a love for him.

As much as gangsters and drug dealers were part of the media portrayal of black life, athletes were a whole other side of the picture. I've heard it said that if music and sports were the only tickets out of the ghetto, not too many brothers would be making the move, and I'd have to agree with that. But even if you're never going to make it as an NBA draft pick, there is still a lot you can learn on the field and the court that you won't get taught anywhere else. Being a team player is important no matter what you might end up doing with your life, and so is playing the game to win. But as much as anything else, sports teaches young black men and women that it's competition that makes you a better person, that striving to be the best is a worthwhile goal no matter if you make the cut or not.

That's what Big Bing was trying to get into my head, anyway, and it was a lesson that went right along with what my mama taught me about believing in myself. To be yourself, you've got to try your best. Nothing else makes any difference. The only one you've got to prove something to is you. Those are truths I carry with me, each day and everywhere I go.

Many of my happiest hours were spent over at Bing's crib, especially when my mama and brothers were there with me. We'd all come over together and, while Mama cooked up dinner in the kitchen, we men would sit around and talk about whatever game was on TV. We were just like a real family, and I think Big Bing must have felt the same way after a while, because it wasn't too long before he moved over to our apartment and, even though it wasn't exactly legal, I felt as good about it as I can ever remember feeling.

Of course, the problem with most good things is that they turn out to be temporary, unless someone's working to keep them going. Big Bing may have been good at playing house with my mama, but when it came time to get serious about raising a family with three young boys, he decided one day he couldn't be a part of that. There was nothing tying him down, exactly—at least not a marriage license or a mortgage payment—so it probably wasn't as hard for him as for someone who had a real commitment. But, when you're a little boy, looking for the guidance and protection and simple love that are supposed to come from a father, you don't care too much about what's convenient or legal or excusable. You just need someone to look up to. Big Bing didn't live up to that need and while you could say he did the best he could with what he had, you could also say that it wasn't enough for the ones who needed him most.

I was around seven years old when Bing took off, and I sure don't remember anyone wasting a lot of tears watching him go. I told myself we were better off without him and maybe, in the long run, that was true. Big Bing just drifted through our lives and when he was gone, we still had to carry on, with or without him.

Like I said, I'll always be grateful to Big Bing for bringing me up as far as he did. And sports is something that I'm still deep into, even today. But the *real* lesson he taught me was when I saw what he didn't do. Then, when my time came, and I had kids of my own, I could make the application. Directly. Spanky and Little Snoop need a full-time father, and no matter what else I may decide to do and not do, that's one job I'll never take for granted. It's the number one priority in my life.

With Big Bing gone, I tried my best to keep up with all the changes and twists of fate that were coming my way. For a little while, anyway, things seemed to settle down around me and I was able to get into a regular routine of growing and getting by. It wasn't too long after he left that we moved into a house on Lewis Avenue and, a little while past that, to another place on Corrine Street. In both of them, I had to share a room with my brother Jerry, and without a father around, he filled in for the next best thing. We did our share of fighting and fussing, just kids' stuff, really, but when it came down to blood ties, Jerry was always there for me, keeping me out of trouble on the playground and watching to see I didn't overstep my place on the street.

Sometimes, though, the both of us were there to help each other get into trouble, like stealing Tootsie Rolls and red licorice from the corner liquor store every morning on the way to school. One morning, as we were on our way out the door with a pocketful of candy, Jerry got caught red-handed, but before they could lay hold of me, I was out the door, down the street, and up the alley.

I ended up going to school like nothing happened, but when I got home that afternoon my mama laid into me something fierce, even though I kept crying and shouting that I hadn't done anything wrong. And in my mind, I hadn't. It was *Jerry* who got caught, not me. And as long as I got away with the goods, it was like I was innocent. Needless to say, my mama didn't see it that way, and after I got my whipping, I got mad all over again, thinking that Jerry had told on me. Of course, he hadn't. He didn't need to. Mamas just know about things like that, like some kind of sixth sense.

From as early as I can remember, I had a big mouth and didn't think twice about shooting it off whenever and wherever I got the urge. Jerry had to bail me out of the trouble I'd gotten into, bragging on myself or dissing someone bigger and badder than my skinny ass would ever hope to be, but I was able to pay back the favor when it came to school-work.

I'm not claiming I was any smarter than Jerry, but when I put my mind to it, I had a natural aptitude when it came to school, and a lot of time I would do his homework for him, even though he was a couple of grades ahead of me.

Because we moved around a lot, I went to a bunch of different schools—Roosevelt, Lafayette, Cleveland—and at each one I was able to find my place back into the books and classes without too much bother. The subjects I liked the best, English and history, were the ones where I got to go to the library and research the facts for myself. There was something about discovering the truth on your own, without anybody telling you, that made it stick with me a little harder and longer, and what I really got into was trying to find answers to questions I would only ask myself. *Where did I come from? Why am I here? What was here before me?* That kind of shit, and although I never did solve too many of those riddles, looking for the answer made me think about things in a different way. Truth, I decided, was never just handed to you. You had to go and find it out for yourself. That's what made it all the more valuable when you finally did dig it up. You might forget what somebody tells you is true. But you're never going to forget what you find out for yourself.

chapter
three

Me with two of my favorit
people—Larry and Jackie
Rogers.

chapter three

Life isn't always about the big, dramatic shit that happens to you when you least expect it. It isn't the shocks and sorrows that make someone into who he is, not even the joy and happiness that comes along every once in a while.

The way I see it, life is about the little things, what you don't notice, what's in the normal and regular run of your days and weeks, all the details that, when you add them together, make up who you are and what you're about.

Check it out: I've had enough excitement and action in my life to last me until I'm old and gray. And if I think about those times when it seemed like everything was hanging in the balance, when I could either win or lose it all, I can still remember that feeling in the pit of my stomach, like the floor had just fallen out under me and my heart was hammering against my ribs like it was trying to break out and fly off—I tell you what, I'm not down for that, ever again. Right at those moments, I was shit-scared. Anyone would be, and if they tell you otherwise, they're lying like a motherfucker. Life is a precious thing. It hangs by a thread, with you tied up to one end and the other end held between God's thumb and finger. He can let go any time He wants and there's nothing you get to say or do about it.

But most of the time, most of us don't sit around thinking on how

God can snap our string any time He gets mad or bored or needs another angel in heaven or another demon in hell. Most of the time, if we're honest, we don't give a thought to any of that metaphysical shit. We think, somewhere deep down inside, that we're just going to keep on living, forever and ever, amen.

Why not? Look around you. Most likely, things are the same today as they were yesterday and, if they're not, they probably will be by tomorrow. The way to play the game is to remind yourself, as much as you can, how lucky you are just to be alive. And that goes for the rap superstar as much as for the brother biding his time on death row. You got to look at what you've been given—the opportunities and the possibilities and the chance to start fresh every day. If you can get grateful for what you've got, and not resent everything that didn't come your way, you might have a whole new regard for the world, and where your ass is situated in it.

That's how youngsters are. You give a kid the toy he wants, you might as well give him a million dollars. He's just as happy. He doesn't know what he's missing and that's why he never thinks he's missing anything. The little homey's got everything he needs, because he's happy with what he's got.

That's the way it was for me coming up, too. I might have wanted that ColecoVision for Christmas, or a fistful of those Tootsie Rolls on the candy counter at the liquor store, but none of it ever made the difference in being sad or happy, the way only a kid can be happy. My life back then was filled up with things that gave me joy, and there's times even now that I wish I could go back to that simple way of living, to appreciate everything I've got and give myself props for getting it in the first place.

For instance, nothing gave me a bigger thrill when I was a kid than when Mama would pile us all in her beat-up old Camaro and drive us down to Norm's Restaurant at Long Beach Boulevard and Pacific Coast Highway for dinner in one of those big, plush red leatherette booths. And if we didn't go to Norm's I was just as happy at the Bonanza, tearing into a big old cheeseburger and getting sloppy with the ketchup. And if we didn't go out at all, I still had Mama's chicken wings and macaroni and cheese to look forward to, specially prepared by the best cook on the east side of Long Beach, at least in my humble opinion.

The money Mama made working two jobs, cleaning in a convalescent home and serving food in a high school cafeteria, didn't go far with three sons, but you could never tell that by me. When she'd take us all out, once a year, for a day at the state fair in Pomona, we might as well have been going to Cancun or the south of fucking France, on an all-expenses paid vacation. When she'd get us all down to Zody's or Gemco to buy us a new pair of Toughskins, the ones with the big old pads stitched in the knees, we might as well have been going to Pierre Cardin for a custom-fitted silk suit. Or when she'd drop us off at the barber shop and tell the man to give us the fattest afro he had, just like the Jacksons or that cute little Arnold on *Diff'rent Strokes,* we might as well have been getting styled by Vidal Motherfuckin' Sassoon.

And not only was I the best-fed, best-dressed, best-looking homey east of Twentieth Street, I had the best, most together and coolest crew of anybody on the playground. Even though my 'hood was exclusively brothers, the schools I went to were integrated, with all kinds of kids bused in from all over Los Angeles to keep the racial balance in line. We had Vietnamese, Samoans, Chicanos, West Side whites . . . any color you care to name. But there was no doubt who was out front and in charge of the jungle gym and the sandbox—the niggers.

It's the truth. Kids looked up to us because of the way we dressed and the way we talked and the way we carried ourselves. It's the same today as it was back then. Brothers invented what's cool and everybody else just follows along. Music, fashion, lifestyle—black is the bomb, and if that sounds arrogant or insolent to you, then you can kiss my black ass.

And of all the little crews, the one I ran with was the dopest, hands down. We had Marcus Crow and Keith Jackson, James Burton and Damian Jones, Rayshon and Junior Haggerty, and every one of those dudes I was proud to call a friend.

But the one I remember the best, the one that really made life sweet, was my very first homegirl, Angie Bishop. She lived down the street from me and we used to walk to school together every morning, never saying much, just digging on each other. You could call us boyfriend and girlfriend, because I was a boy and she was a girl, but it really didn't go any further than that. We were too young to know exactly what to do with what we had, but even if we did, I don't think it would have come to that. We were friends, first, foremost, and finally, and being romantic or sexual in any kind of way, even a kiss, would just have spoiled that.

I felt like I could tell Angie anything, even though, at eight years old, it wasn't exactly like I had a lot of secrets I was holding back. But just knowing she was there, straight and up front and on my side, gave me a good feeling. She had the darkest brown eyes that seemed to gather up all the sunlight that came up over the houses in the morning as we walked our route to school, and when she smiled it was like someone had turned on a hundred-watt bulb. Angie was something else.

It's been my experience that women can make the best friends a homeboy can have. With brothers, a lot of times it's a macho thing. They're all about what you got and how they can get some for themselves. But a female, she can just be happy *for* you, without getting all jealous and trying to make herself look good in your eyes. I've had a lot of true friends that are women with nothing sexual attached, and no thought even given to it. When I first got married my wife didn't exactly understand or approve of that situation, but as she got to know me better and could check out the sisters I had around me, she was eventually cool with it. That's one of the reasons she's the best friend I've got today.

Coming up, I've got to say that I had an eye out for the ladies from a very early age. There were two or three of them in my church youth group that I'd be checking out instead of paying attention to the sermon and later, when I got higher up in school, it was like my duty as a homeboy to try and get next to as many of the little foxes as I could. I didn't have my game down the way other brothers did, but that didn't stop me from trying, and I figure, back in the day, I was running about a 35 percent rejection ratio, which wasn't bad for a kid who wasn't quite sure what he was supposed to do with a sister when he got one. I was just happy if they'd be giving me the time of day, and if I could talk them into going to a movie or maybe spending a couple hours up at the Fox Hills Mall looking into store windows and drinking Orange Julius, then I figured I must be doing it right.

It wasn't until I was twelve years old that I finally put it all together and got instructed in how to put tab A into slot B. And when my cherry *did* get popped, I didn't mess around. I had two girls teaching me to bump at the same time.

I was chilling at the house of one of them up on Twenty-third Street one day after school when it was real hot and we had the curtains pulled in her bedroom, all alone in the house with her mama out working and her brothers and sisters playing out on the street. I can still remember hearing their laughing and shouting through the window where we were sitting in the dark, playing around with each other with no serious direction in mind. One thing might have been leading to another, but if we were heading somewhere, I sure enough didn't know how to get there. I just liked feeling her smooth, warm skin and the way she put her hand inside my pants and started feeling around like she was looking for hidden candy. She had a way of putting her tongue halfway down my throat when we kissed and it gave me a feeling somewhere between giggling and gagging, like I wanted her to stop and keep going all at the same time.

We must have been at it in there about a half hour when the door creaked open and somebody moved up alongside the bed and started giggling. I about jumped out of my skin with embarrassment, but then I saw that it was only another homegirl from down the block. The two of them started laughing together then, pointing at me, standing in the corner with my pants down around my ankles, and that was getting me mad, so I started cussing them out and they started laughing even harder and pretty soon we were all back on the bed, only this time they both had their hands in my pants, with one's tongue in my mouth and the other's in my ear.

I don't know where they learned to do all that shit, but I wasn't about to stop them, especially when they started taking off their clothes and rubbing against me, one on either side. Then, without exactly knowing how, they got me all moved around into the right position; I was suddenly on top of one of them, with the other kind of sitting on the sidelines coaxing us along and giving us pointers. I couldn't tell you which was which, but it didn't matter much anyway, because after a while they switched places and it was about then that I started getting that strange feeling down between my legs. Then, all of a sudden, it was like everything just let go and I heard a yelp that made me jump all over again until I realized it was me making noise and I rolled off whoever I was spread out on and just lay there for a minute, breathing hard and watching the sparks in front of my eyes go off in all directions.

The two of them took to giggling again and I could still hear the youngsters outside playing hide-and-seek, but I wasn't paying much attention to anything right about then. I knew that I'd just had sex for the first time, and as far as I was concerned, it might just as well have been the last. I felt weak and tired and a little sick to my stomach and I was thinking that if this was what everybody was getting so excited about and trying to get a piece of, like they were going to die if they didn't have some first thing in the morning and last thing at night, well, then, they were welcome to it. I preferred sports.

No shit. It was going to take me a while to get used to sex, to get to that place where I was actually enjoying it, but out on the playing field, it was like I was right where I belonged, from jump. I loved hoops, mostly from watching the Lakers with Big Bing, and while I definitely had the height, I wasn't fast enough to really hold my own on the court.

But football was a whole other story. There's hardly a time in my life when I don't remember playing the game in one style or another, starting when I was just a youngster, and we'd play head-to-head out on the street. We didn't pay much attention to rules—scrimmages or downs or penalties. We'd just lay the ball in the middle of the block and go at it, slugging it up and knocking each other over and trying to hold on until somebody grabbed it and ran it home and then we'd start all over again.

But by the time I got into school and got interested in what you might call the finer points of the game, I realized I had some skills I could bring to bear. I could use my height to passing advantage, and I was quick enough on my feet that I could run that thing home myself if I had to, so by the time I was eight years old, I was playing Pop Warner football as the quarterback and really working my game to the max. The team was the Long Beach Rough Riders, and we had what it took to make it to two championship games and walk home with the trophy in one of them.

At that time, I guess I was like most everyone else in the ghetto, dreaming about a pro ball career, but I kept getting told that, because I didn't have enough meat on my skinny ass, there was no way I could get a break. I knew that was bullshit even back then, and today, when I see all these little brothers in the NBA or the NFL, brothers skinnier than I am, I'm even more sure that it's never about size or speed or some kind of class-A athletic credentials. Playing sports, and being good at what you play, is all about heart. Always was and always will be. I had what it took, because I loved the game and I had the utmost confidence in my ability to play. If someone else had believed in me like I believed in myself, you might be reading a whole different story today, the story of a sports hero. But, like I said, God had something else in mind.

But word: God used football to teach me about life, and not even so much the game's strategy and discipline and teamwork—that shit any brother can use to improve himself. What I'm talking about is the faith to believe in yourself, to know that God is on your side and that He cares about you trying the best you can, no matter who you are.

The man who used to teach me those lessons, one on one, was Coach Johnson, who was behind all our success in the Pop Warner league. He was a good coach, with a natural understanding of the game and the ability to inspire and motivate his players. But that wasn't what made him one of the most important influences in my life. It was the fact that the coach kept pointing us back to God, showing us by example what it meant to have a mission and to follow through on that mission. For the four years I was in the Rough Riders, the coach would pick me up from home to drive me to almost every practice. He'd lead us in prayer before every game. And after every game, too. He gave as much personal attention and instruction to the worst youngblood on the team as he did to the best, not like most coaches who focus on their star players and let everyone else figure shit out for themselves. He was a man who really cared about us, in a world where we didn't have too many men who would take the time and effort to show us what life was about and how to win at the game. That's something you don't forget, and all I can say is I hope you all have got somebody like that standing solid next to you when it counts. God works through the people He brings into your life, and Coach Johnson was a man God handpicked to help a bunch of ragged-ass kids in East Long Beach to get through.

The sad part is, some of us learned the lesson and some of us didn't. I stayed in the game right through my high school years and made my mark on the athletic program of every team I played on. But it was those days in the Pop Warner league, with Coach Johnson, that I remember best of all. It wasn't too long ago that I came across a picture of the Rough Riders when we first got together, all of us looking proud and happy in our fresh new uniforms, with the coach standing behind like he was proud of himself just to show us off. It when I started going down those rows of faces, counting off what happened to all my teammates, that I realized for the first time what a hard job the coach really had, trying to stand between us and all the shit that was starting to tear our 'hood apart.

From right to left, most of the brothers in that picture were either dead, on dope, or on death row. It was like looking at a gallery of ghosts, their lives wasted before they even had a chance to live them.

chapter four

Stylin' and profilin' at the pro
Me in high school.

chapter four

a brother who tells you that he knows why some things change and some things stay the same, why the best of times can turn bad and the worst of times turn out okay—that brother's just blowing smoke up your ass. No one knows the ways of God, what His purpose down here on earth is, and the best we can do is to be truthful to what we know is right and don't let anything keep us from walking that path . . . in the good times or the bad.

When things started changing in the 'hood, none of us could exactly put our finger on the why and what for of it all. It just seemed like one day the people around you were full of hope, expecting something better from life and waiting on that eventuality. And the next day, those same people gave up their hope, didn't expect anything to ever be any different from what it was, and stopped waiting for a change to come.

I might be exaggerating, but not by that much. It didn't all happen in one day, not even in a month or a year, but when it did happen it was final and for sure—no doubt about it. It was like the spirit got sucked out of the 'hood, like the hard times and poverty we'd learned to live through got to be more than any of us could overlook anymore. We lost our dream, and when the dream was gone, we got mad, and when we got mad enough we started taking it out on each other.

Maybe that's the way generations change, the way the youngbloods see things different than their elders, who always want to talk about "back in the day" like things shouldn't ever be any different than when they were coming up. The sixties were before my time, but I've studied up enough to know that those were years when brothers really believed things could be different and that everyone could make a difference by putting themselves on the line and standing up for the cause. Then the seventies came, my time, and that hope and faith in a better day was still alive. We could look around and measure our progress, see brothers and sisters on TV and in the movies, running businesses, making scrilla for them and their families, and leading the way out of the ghetto. But after a while, it was just like anything else you've got to wait around for too long. At first you're all pumped up, expecting you'll be getting what you want before too much longer. Then, when it doesn't come around, you start losing your cool, and pretty soon you've got a beef with the world, and you don't even care if it ever comes or not. As a matter of fact, you start hoping it *doesn't* show up, because all you want to do is find the motherfucker who put your dreams on hold and pop a cap on him. You want *revenge,* payback for all the disappointment and disillusionment you've been going through, and that's when all the peace and love turns to hate and violence and twenty years later you got the L.A. riots with Reginald Denny and Rodney King and all the other shit that comes down when society gets sick in its soul and turns on itself like a snake eating its tail.

For my money, this is what the eighties were about and what caused the problems of the nineties. And there's more than enough blame to go around. Sure enough, Ronald Reagan was an asshole who didn't give a fuck about the poor black man and cut off all the programs that helped the brothers get through. But what about the niggers themselves? None of them ever want to cop to the hard truth that it wasn't some politician that burned down the ghetto, got all the bitches pregnant and all the youngsters hooked on crack. That was us, doing it to ourselves, and whether or not we had the right to be pissed off about our treatment from slave days right on through to O.J., it was still no one else but *us* doing the damage to ourselves and in the end someone has got to take responsibility for being a man in a man's world. So let it start here, with Snoop Dogg—father, family man, and motherfucking role model for a whole other generation of youngbloods coming up hard behind me.

All of us are going to have hard times in our lives. Guaranteed. It's not whether you have them, it's what you do about them when they come along. They can kill you or they can make you stronger, and this is one nigger who's still standing. You can take that to the bank.

I can't put my finger on exactly when it was that things starting turning bad on the streets of East Long Beach. But I do know that whatever was happening out there was also happening to us as a family. It might have just been the fact of my growing up, noticing things for the first time that I'd been too young and innocent to pick up on before. But whatever it was, when those simple and straight-ahead times of my early days started fading away, there was nothing that could bring them back.

I've heard it said that drugs were what destroyed ghetto society and corrupted all the values that kept families together. I've got no dispute with that, except to say that drugs and alcohol were always a part of life on the street for as long as I can remember and way before anybody ever heard of crack cocaine. Some of the closest times I ever had with my mama was when she and I had our own little spur-of-the-moment parties, listening to her records and drinking beer together. I couldn't have been more than eight years old at the time, but I never thought anything of sucking a Colt 45 or a Mickey's Big Mouth on a hot summer day listening to the O'Jays or the Stylistics do their thing. Mama didn't see anything wrong with it either, and to this day, I think she enjoyed those drinking times with me as much as any partying she did with her boyfriends. After we knocked back a few, we'd get to laughing and carrying on and we'd start dancing around together and it was those times when I felt like my mama's special child, like we shared something that nobody else was a part of.

Same thing with chronic. My mother's brother Marvin used to come around the crib every once in a while and he and I would sit out in the backyard and share one of those big fat blunts he'd roll up with that homegrown shit of his. We'd get a good buzz on and the afternoon would just kind of drift along in that no-hassle zone where everything is cool and nothing can mess with your head until someone next door would start cooking up some barbecue and get you so hungry you'd have to get your ass up and eat a half dozen peanut butter sandwiches or a box of Cheerios or whatever else you can grab in the kitchen that your mama hadn't nailed down. Those were good times.

And when they were over, you just knew they weren't coming back. My uncle Marvin would move on from pot to pills and it wasn't too long before he turned up dead of an overdose. Another one of my mother's brothers killed himself along with his girlfriend, for reasons that seemed all the more scary because none of us knew exactly what they were. One minute these people were up alongside your life, filling a familiar space in your everyday routine, and the next minute they were only as real as your memory of them. Suddenly death wasn't something that happened to people on TV shows anymore. My own family members were checking out and nobody could tell me why.

Other shit was changing, too, and none of it was good. After Mama and Big Bing went their separate ways, she hooked up with a couple of niggers that I had no use for whatsoever. The first one's name was Billy and they ended up getting married for a couple of years until she caught on to what kind of bad news he really was and cut him loose. But before that happened, I had to make my own moves toward becoming the man of the house and protecting my mama and my little brother. Billy, it turned out, was a heavy drinker who spent all his time sitting around the crib with a big tall glass tipped to the top with Jack or Turkey, and when he got drunk, he got mean. It was all a part of that out-of-control feeling that was taking hold in those days. Time was when my mama and me could share a six-pack and get nothing worse than happy, but this motherfucker would sit around hoping for a reason to slap someone upside the head and if he couldn't find one, he'd make one up. He and my mama were always fussing and fighting and sometimes it would get so bad I'd have to split, just to chill over at one of my homies' until they wore themselves out. Other times, Billy would threaten us kids and that would get my mama all worked up and they'd start in on each other all over again.

After a couple of years Mama divorced Billy, not that she really needed to, since he'd taken to living with one or another of his bitches, anyway. But she just wanted to make it official, mostly because she found someone else, a brother named Michael who at first seemed like a big improvement over Billy. But that's not saying much for either one of them, to tell the motherfucking truth of the matter.

I first I liked Michael well enough, mostly because he took my side in the fights I was having at that time with my mama. At twelve years old, I was ready to try out a few things on my own, staying up as late as I wanted, coming home all hours, hanging with my homies. But to Mama, I was still her little baby and she was always laying down the law, giving me a nine o'clock curfew and telling me exactly what she thought of my friends.

But Michael was always after her to loosen up the apron strings a little, to let us kids do our thing and find out on our own what was what. I appreciated that, even though now I sometimes wonder if he wasn't just saying all that to get us out of the house. But it didn't matter anyway, because it wasn't too long until he started showing his true colors, doing that lowlife shit that was getting only too common in the ghetto.

Now, it was around then that I'd taken to living out of the house pretty much all the time, so I didn't actually see any of the moves Michael pulled going down firsthand. But news travels fast in the 'hood, and when it got round to me, I got together a posse and we drove around after dark looking for Michael until we finally tracked him down and whopped his ass.

I thought that was all there was to it until the next day, when I heard that this time he was on the prowl for *me*. All of a sudden that posse I'd pulled together was nowhere to be found. The truth is, I was nothing but a youngster trying to protect his mama and now I had this big motherfucker out hunting me down. It's the kind of thing a kid in the ghetto might go to his father to fix, but, of course, I didn't have a father to go to. So I did the next best thing. Ducking and weaving through back alleys, I got myself over to where Billy—my mama's ex-husband— was chilling and told him about the situation. Before I knew it, he'd pulled out the biggest, baddest gat I'd ever seen and swore he was going blow Michael away if he so much as laid another finger on any of us.

Feeling a lot more confident all of a sudden, we cruised the 'hood to smoke Michael out and, in one of those high noon scenes like out of a western, we found him, drinking beer on a corner with some of his homies. Billy drew down on him, told him to back off, and gave him a pistol whipping to prove his point. After it was all over, I'd have to say I didn't feel so proud about having a drunk like Billy doing my enforcing, but I also didn't feel so bad about having Michael out of my life either.

Problem was, he didn't stay gone for long, and this time it was my mama to blame for taking him back. I wouldn't say it was her fault exactly—trying to raise a family of boys on her own couldn't have been easy, and having a man to hold up some of that load, even a man who thought he had the right to disrespect her, must have been a hard choice to turn down. But, for me, the choices she was making were more than I could handle. When I heard he was back living with her, I got her alone and laid down the law: unless she got rid of Michael, she was going to lose a son. I couldn't tell you who I thought I was back then, other than just a young punk kid trying to throw his weight around, but I meant it. I respected her too much to stand around helpless while she got punched and slapped and kicked, and it was better for me not to see her at all than to see her under those conditions. So I up and moved out for good.

Fact is, there wasn't much room left for me in that place, anyway. It wasn't too long after that whole scene went down that my mama had taken in a little baby boy as part of the family. He'd been born to my uncle and his girlfriend, the ones that ended up killing themselves, and the mother had been into shine pretty heavy, so the baby was sick from jump and needed lots of care and attention. First off, he'd gone into a home, been given up for adoption, and been taken in by this white family across town until he was about two years old. But my mama didn't feel right about leaving one of our own flesh and blood in the hands of strangers, so she petitioned the court and, since she was the youngster's aunt, they handed over custody.

My cousin's name was Martin, and I always felt a special connection with him, probably because, to begin with, we had the same birthday. Martin really loved that white family he had been a part of, and when he first came to live with us, he used to cry himself to sleep every night, asking for his mama and daddy. As far as he knew, that was where he belonged, and black and white didn't have a thing to do with it.

Seeing as how he was so attached to his white family, my mama made sure we stayed in touch with them, and for a while there, this whole white crew would show up to celebrate my and Martin's birthday together. It wasn't until he got a little older that he began to see the difference between them and us and shied away from the people who had given him his start. To this day, I can't say whether it was right or wrong to take little Martin out of that home and away from the parents who loved him so much. Maybe it would have come to the point where he realized he didn't fit into that white world. But it's just as possible that he might have found his way in that world. All I know is we tried to give him as much love and support as we could, and in the end, I can only hope that it made a difference.

Looking back, I guess I'd have to say that with Martin in the house, I felt a little easier about moving out and giving up my place as Mama's baby boy. She had someone else to take care of now. I had done my part to watch out for her and protect her, sometimes even from the mistakes she made herself, like hooking back up with that motherfucker Michael. Now that she had someone to take care of full time, someone who needed her as much as I once had, I figured she wouldn't miss me so much, and I wouldn't miss her.

But there was coming a time when I would have given anything just to go back and be her special little homeboy, even if it was only for one more day. And that time was coming up fast. Things were changing quicker than I could keep track of them, and life in Long Beach was turning hard and mean. Whatever was left over from the sixties—all that optimism about the future and those big dreams of equality and justice and peace on the streets—was getting swallowed up by drugs and guns and war between the races.

It was a bad time to be a young nigger, on your own and out on the streets, but you couldn't tell that to me. I just wanted the chance to prove myself, to make my reputation and stand tall in the 'hood, no matter what it took. It took just about everything I had. And it gave nothing back.

Ready or not, it was time for Snoop Dogg to grow up. My days as an innocent youngster were over and I wouldn't be getting my role models from *Good Times* and *Fat Albert* anymore. There was a whole new class of hero coming up—the pimp and the outlaw, the thug and the gangster—and if you wanted to stay alive on the streets of Long Beach or Watts or Compton or anywhere else where the American Dream was falling apart and fading away, you better get with their program. It was the only game in town.

chapter five

Banging with the L.B.C.

chapter five

Loyalty is the number one quality required for life in the ghetto. I know what I'm talking about. Your first priority is to find someone you trust to watch your back, cover your game, and keep you honest. Without that, you're as good as gone the minute you step out on your own. It doesn't take a Ph.D. to figure out that gangs are what give you that sense of security, but even in a gang, there's got to be one homey who you *know* will go to the wall for you, just like you'd go to the wall for him.

For me, that position was taken by my main man, my truest and longest-running homeboy, Warren G. He's been tight with me since the beginning, and more times than I care to count, he saved my sorry ass. Just the same as I saved his. Growing up, there's nobody closer than him in my heart.

I'd even go so far as to say that if it wasn't for G, I wouldn't have ever made it as a rapper. There was a lot of times when I just didn't believe in myself and my skills, when I thought that my flow was worthless and my rhymes no better than what you'd read in Mother Goose. At times like that, I'd gather up all my papers and notebooks and toss them in nearest garbage can. It was always G who fished them back out and kept them in a safe place until I got my confidence back to give it another try. When nobody else cared, he hung in with me, and when I didn't have enough reliance on myself, he'd have it for me.

I first met Warren when I was six and he was seven, and we'd spot each other hanging out in Martin Luther King Park, taking part in the recreation programs they had set up there for youngsters with nowhere else to go. We even played some Pop Warner football together one season and his daddy, who was a football coach out in Compton, would drop around every once in a while and give us some pointers. G had two older sisters and a younger one, Missy, who went to school with me. They all lived with their mama a half block away from our crib.

But what really brought G and me together was when we got teamed up to sell candy. I still remember how it went down. We were all at the swimming pool in King Park one hot summer day when this nigger drove up in a van and started talking to the youngbloods hanging out around the snack bar. He asked us if we were interested in making some money, which was a dumb question to put to poor kids, anyway, but we played along and told him what he wanted to hear, just to find out his game.

This brother, whose name, if I remember right, was Jeff, picked out a half dozen or so of us, including me and G, and we all got into his van. He drove us out to some white neighborhood, with big wide lawns and sprinklers spraying water and making rainbows up against the blue sky. He gave us each a sack full of candy—bags of Jolly Ranchers and Hershey's Kisses and boxes of Almond Joy and Snickers and all that other shit that makes a kid's eyes get big and his grille fall out. Jeff sent us all out in different directions with our booty and we went door to door the rest of the afternoon, selling sweets to white folks who must have felt sorry for the ragged-ass little black kids hustling candy on a hot day. That afternoon we met back at the van, turned in our money, and got our cut. The truth was, we all made out pretty well, at least by our thirteen-year-old way of looking at it.

We spent the rest of the summer riding all around L.A. in the back of that van, selling candy in 'hoods from Costa Mesa to Palos Verdes to Beverly Hills, and it wasn't too long before G and I teamed up to cover two sides of one block at same time.

It was during those months that we really got to know each other, let each other in on all our little juvenile dreams and secrets and got solid with a friendship that has lasted right up to this day. I'd have to say that

Warren G knows more about me than any other nigger alive, and that includes my mama and my wife. The same goes for him, too. He trusted me with shit he'd *never* tell anyone else, because he knows I'm there for him like he's there for me. That kind of connection is worth its weight in solid gold.

It was also during those times, walking up and down those big broad avenues, with a backpack full of melting chocolate on our shoulders, that G and I discovered a common love for old-school R&B and the new sound that was just starting to make itself felt around then. They called it rap.

Now, both G and I were of the opinion that rap was coming along just in time to give the brothers a new musical direction to follow. It had been too long since soul had made any real noise, longer still since R&B had gotten anybody excited. Black music back in the early eighties was more or less on hold, waiting for something to shake niggers up and get them back where they belonged—which was right out front, showing the whites which way to go. All that break dancing shit combined with Michael Jackson and a lot of tired old retreads doing their thing was about all we had to offer before rap, but once the real stuff showed up, it was like the world got turned upside down.

Check it out—today, hip-hop music sells more records than R&B or soul ever did; it sells more than country and Latin and jazz combined; it sells more than motherfucking *rock & roll,* and that's no bullshit. Rap is the hottest music of our time and there's a good reason for it. It's real. It talks about the way things *are,* not just the way they ought to be. Like back in the sixties, when they had protest music, those songs gave people a clue about what was really going down around them, got them motivated to go out and do something about it. Rap has got some of that same purpose, but it's about a whole lot more than just complaining over the situation. Rap is an answer in itself, a way for the niggers to make a noise, get noticed, and scare the shit out of a lot of motherfuckers who've been trying to pretend that, if they don't pay us any attention, maybe we'd just go away. Well, we're here to stay! Rap music proves that and has been proving it for going on twenty years, with no sign of slowing down.

Back when G and I were first getting tuned into the sound, rap wasn't

about East Coast and West Coast; it wasn't about pimps and whores; and it sure wasn't about cop killers and gangstas. Brothers just didn't have the nerve to put that stuff out there yet. Most of them—rappers like Real Gang, Whodini, Run-D.M.C. and the Fat Boys—were busy trying to lay out the new turf and get themselves a foothold in the music business. Some of them had their successes, but the word back then was that rap was just a fad that was already on its way out. It was only a matter of time before something else came along to take its place.

G and I knew better. Just by instinct we realized that rap, which was nothing more than putting rhyming words behind a beat, was going to change everything. We just had no idea how popular the sound was going to get and how it was going to change our lives, for better and for good.

But as much as rap may have just been a novelty back in the day, there were already signs that this wasn't business as usual. You just had to know where to look. Sure enough, nobody was coming down yet on that East–West rivalry tip that was sooner or later going to get pumped all out of proportion in the media. The straight-up fact was that in L.A. we just didn't have the kind of rap acts that could make a difference nationally. All the action was back east, or at least that's where all the biggest stars and the hottest labels were making a name for themselves.

Out west it was different. Outside their own turf, no one had heard of most of the local talent, and if you ever picked up on a West Coast record, it would mostly likely be on some little sorry-ass label that some brother was running out of his garage. We couldn't compete with our rivals across the country, who were getting the sweet major-label deals and seeing their videos on MTV and their records in heavy rotation.

From my point of view, it was this same situation that made West Coast rap as powerful as it was when it finally got the attention it deserved. The homies didn't have to deal with selling out, compromising their message, or getting ripped off by the record industry before they ever had a chance to do their thing. West Coast rap had room to *breathe,* and the best of the brothers—like Ice T., L.A. Dreamteam, and, of course, the Wreckin' Cru'—didn't have to worry about whether their shit could hit until they'd already proved it by building up a base from right out of the 'hood. That's the way the game should be played, anyway—forget the hype, and let the sound find its own way around.

That way, you know for sure if what you're dealing with is for real.

Like everyone else back in the day, G and I were out looking for what was real, and if we couldn't find it, we figured we'd make the shit happen by ourselves. It's that same attitude that makes rap so different from most other kinds of music. If you think you got what it takes, there's nothing stopping you from giving it a shot. You don't need a music degree, or ten years of saxophone lessons or a forty-eight-track studio to bust a move. It comes down to two things: your skills and your balls. Almost anybody can find something to rhyme. It takes a rapper to put a message to his words, and that means you've got to have the courage of your convictions. Say what you mean. Mean what you say. It sounds simple. But it will take everything you've got to give.

G and I would try out raps on each other during those long afternoons walking around those rich white streets, flowing on anything and everything we could think of, and most times it didn't mean shit. What have two thirteen-year-old niggers got to tell anybody, anyway? But that wasn't what we were about. We just liked the sound of our own voices. We liked cracking each other up with stories about the little everyday things that happened in our lives, putting ourselves into the plots of movies and TV shows, or just dreaming out loud about all the fine scrilla we'd put together with what we'd earned at the end of the day.

And for my money, that was some of the best rapping I ever did, even to this day. It was all free and easy back then, just letting myself go where the words wanted to take me, surprising myself and my homeboy with the funny way I could twist a line to come together right where it was supposed to, taking a word from the top of the verse and putting it at the end just to keep my flow in form. Those earliest days was when I really first started to get my style in shape. It seemed like most of the rappers that we heard wanted to get it all out in one breath, rhyming as fast and furious as they could, like if they didn't say it right then and there, they were never going to get another chance.

I took a different approach, slowing things down a bit, giving myself a lot of room to maneuver, coming up on the rhythm from a different angle and putting as much into the spaces between the words as into the words themselves. I can't say I was doing what I did on purpose. I never considered myself as some kind of West Coast answer to the East

Coast style. I just did what fit my personality, and niggers that know me will tell you I don't like to be hurried. I've got an easy loping style of walking and talking and bumping and that suits me just fine. When I started rapping it only made sense to let up off the accelerator and get a little backstroke working.

From jump, though, Warren could tell that I was onto something. G had his own skills, though to tell the truth, he wasn't a natural when it came to freestyling. He'd tell you that himself. But he never got jealous of what I was doing, or tried to diss my ability just to make himself look good. Like I said, G is my number one homeboy. He was back then . . . he still is today.

That nigger was there 100 percent to support and encourage me. After a day selling candy, on the way back to Long Beach in the back of Jeff's van, he put together these spur-of-the-moment rap contests, putting me up against whoever thought they was hot from the other crews. And, like I said, when I'd get discouraged and disgusted with myself, G was there to give me the boost up I needed to keep it going on.

But it wasn't that G was just wishing me luck and keeping his fingers crossed. My man was connected, and he made the best of those connections to help me out. See, G had a half brother over in Compton who went by the name Dr. Dre. At the time, Dre was making some noise around L.A. with his group the Wreckin' Cru', and they were about as close as any of us got to a real live rap artist.

But Dre was more than just some amateur motherfucker looking to break out. From the get, the Doctor had the phattest skills of anyone on the West Coast, hands down. I should know, I've worked with some of the hottest producers in the world on my records, and also some who *thought* they were the hottest, but Dre is one of the only stone-cold geniuses I ever stood in the same room with. The nigger just *knew* what to do. He was a perfectionist and a creator and an inspiration to anyone he ever dealt with and you can hear it in the music we made . . . and keep making, right up to the shit we've done together recently. Dr. Dre is a once-in-a-lifetime talent and I've been blessed that he just happened along in my lifetime.

Dre's father had been married for a while to Warren G's mama, and when they split up, he moved out to Compton and found another woman, who was Dre's mama. He and G, being related, kept in touch, even after Dre started making a name for himself with the Wreckin' Cru'.

Now, G is what I call a nagger—always on a brother for one thing or another. He'd just show up at Dre's crib in Compton and nag the motherfucker to death about this skinny-ass friend of his who could rap circles around anyone else in Long Beach. He was always giving me top billing, pumping me up more than I deserved, and I don't blame Dre for shining him on at first. He probably heard the same story twenty times a day from twenty different niggers. What was so special about me? But G kept at it, telling Dre that I was his main homeboy and that he needed to perp with me because I was heading somewhere and it was only a matter of time and all that other bullshit that he could dish up on a platter. And when Dre wouldn't pay any mind, G would toss him one of my homemade tapes, so that when the nigger was kicking it, he might just put my shit on.

He must have kept that up for months, but I think the more he pushed, the more Dre played him off, just because he had his own business to attend to, which wasn't about making niggers from Long Beach famous. After a while, G realized he was going to have to take that job on himself. If he was going to get Dre to give me the time of day, we were going to have to prove we could make some moves on our own.

The only question was, who were we going to get to go along with our grand plan? In school I'd traded some raps with a brother who called himself Domino and we busted some pretty dope moves. But Domino wanted to do his own thing and, since G didn't have all that much confidence as a rapper, we figured it was best to try and pull in some other talent. I had an idea of which nigger I wanted right away. I just wasn't sure how G was going to feel about my candidate.

I met Nate Dogg during my first year of high school, when he and I both played football in what they called the Gospel League, which was made up of teams from different churches around town. He was a couple of years older than me, but we had the same P.E. class and science lab and that's when I first heard him singing, doing songs off the radio before class started and we'd have to dissect some motherfucking frog or something. I figured that with me rapping, Nate singing, and G bringing up the slack, we had a pretty good lineup, but I also knew that G and Nate didn't get along and hadn't from the first time they'd met.

The reason was simple: G was selfish when it came to our friendship. He didn't like anyone else trying to get up close to me and he saw Nate as a threat to our partnership. I tried to tell him that there wasn't anybody who could take his place and that Nate was just another brother from the 'hood with some skills who could help us out, but he wouldn't back down. At least not at first. It wasn't until I got everyone together and we tried out a few things that G cooled off a little and agreed to let Nate be part of the game. But he always kept a sharp eye out after that, making sure of what was what and who was who and where the lines were drawn.

It was cool with me. As far as I was concerned, what mattered most was doing music. And on that count, we were definitely making progress.

chapter six

Checkin' my flow,
circa 1988.

chapter six

the folks that answered their doors along the candy route that G and I walked that summer weren't the only whites I'd come face-to-face with during my early years. Even though the ghetto was a closed-off world when it came to meeting and mixing with other races, I've had more than my share of run-ins with whites and I have to admit, straight up, that sometimes it's like dealing with aliens from another planet.

I know what everyone says, that underneath the skin we're all the same—same hopes and dreams, with good and bad coming in all colors. I wouldn't say that's a lie, not exactly, except that, in my experience, the difference between *them* and *us* is sometimes so wide that we might as well be a completely different kind of animal, from cradle to grave. Black and white have less in common than most of us want to believe— different ways of thinking and acting and looking at reality, and while maybe that doesn't mean we aren't ever going to be able to live together in peace, reaching that goal is going to be a whole lot harder than most of us, black or white, want to accept.

White people, from my way of looking at it, have what you might call an attitude of entitlement. They expect things to come their way, go their way, and get out of their way, and it's hard for them to accept the cold facts when they don't add up to the bottom line they have in mind. A white brother can't help it—he was born thinking certain powers and privileges come with the territory. It's not even like having a chip on your shoulder or a silver spoon in your mouth. It's more like being told you're more special and select and choice from the first moment you can understand what those words mean and you just naturally take all that to heart. So even if you might be no better than poor white trash, you can feel good that there'll always be someone further down the ladder than you are. You might call that point of view just having simple self-esteem and I wouldn't argue the point. White people have got nothing if they don't have self-esteem, even when they don't exactly deserve to feel so good about themselves. That's what comes from being society's top dog for so long—you get to accepting that position as your due, what you deserve and what the rest of the world owes you.

For black people that ain't the name of the game. Don't get me wrong—there's plenty of my brothers and sisters think the world owes them a living. They're just generally not in a position to collect on that debt. Even a middle-class nigger who wants to act like the world is fair and everyone plays by the rules knows deep down that he's got to grab what he wants, then hold on tight and stand ready for a fight to keep it. Equality is about achievement: whoever achieves the most gets treated the most equal. Niggers start out with a disadvantage. It's called racism, and there's no use pretending that it's not out there. I'm not saying that every black man and woman has some obstacle facing them that can't be overcome. If that was true we might as well all just give up now, get back into our slave chains, and start shuffling out to the cotton field.

Whatever we overcome makes us stronger. That's another fact of life. And if we don't try to better ourselves, we've got no one to blame but ourselves. But let's keep it real. All the jobs programs and affirmative action and empowerment zones from here to Harlem don't change the fact that we live in a racist motherfucking society. And that fact puts every black citizen at a disadvantage. A disadvantage we've got to deal with.

How you deal with it depends on you. Speaking just for myself, I'm not really about equal opportunity, a head start, and a level playing field. What I've learned from life in the ghetto is that nothing is for free and if they tell you it is, they're lying. The one who gets ahead is the one who knows that the best way to play the game is when you're the banker, with all the hotels on Boardwalk and a Get-out-of-Jail-Free card up your sleeve. Any advantage you can get is one you should use, and that includes making the most of whatever talents and abilities God gave you. Nobody ever got their ass out of the ghetto by letting someone else step ahead of them in line, and no one ever got rich or famous by laying back and hoping someone would notice who they are and what they do. The streets will teach you about racism and capitalism and the survival of the fittest. Don't worry about that. The only thing you've got to worry about is if you've got enough cold-blooded ambition to apply the lessons you get taught.

That's something a black man knows. It's instinct, born to him, like the color of his skin. No one is entitled to anything except what he can earn, rob, or talk someone else into giving him. It's no wonder pimps and hustlers and gangstas are the heroes of the 'hood. They're the ones that got their props the old-fashioned way—they took them.

I mentioned before about how I used to hang out on the playground with the whites, Latinos, and Asians that would be bused into the 'hood from all around the county. That was probably the first time I got up close and personal with kids from a whole other world, but it worked the other way, too. One year, me and some brothers got selected for a busing program that took us past the invisible boundaries that divide the white part of town from the black. And word: I sure met some sorry-ass folks on that side of the tracks. Seemed like every grown-up I met, every teacher and all the mamas and daddies of the kids in my class, had some kind of guilty trip they were trying to deal with, feeling sorry about being rich and white and having all that good shit in their big mansions with the three-car garage and the built-in barbecue and the Jacuzzi with those little Styrofoam floaters to put your drinks on while you're kicking it naked style in the pool with your wife or that bitch you got stashed in an apartment down on the west side with the nose job and the tit job and the little red Mercedes convertible you'll be making payments on. Seemed to me these assholes were living fucked-up lives, all hidden and full of secrets and feeling bad about not having anything to show for themselves except a pile of cash and a bleeding ulcer.

So, naturally, I did what I could to help them out in their predicament. One of those little white punks would invite me home after school to try out their Atari or whatever else was the fad that week, and the parents would be falling all over themselves to show a real little black kid from the real live ghetto just how open-minded and understanding and racially harmonious they could be, giving me a tall glass of milk and a plate full of Pepperidge Farm Milanos, or having the Filipino cook make up his special hamburger, with some kind of smelly goat cheese on top, and all the while they're smiling and patting me on the head like I was a runaway slave off the plantation. Then we'd go upstairs to play video games until the brat got bored and started watching an after-school special or *Ninja Turtles* or something. And when he was all involved with his favorite turtle, I'd slip out and case the place, snatch up a few souvenirs of my visit—a watch or a Game Boy or some crystal figurine out of a glass cabinet that I knew I could trade back in the 'hood for a bag of chronic or a couple dead presidents. I'd be out in time to catch the school bus, which was my getaway car back to the ghetto.

And none of those whites folks ever said a word about it. You could count on them being so uptight about accusing a poor little disadvantaged black child of lifting their shit that they'd just as soon pretend it never happened and keep on smiling and stroking and telling themselves what a good deed they'd done.

My opinion of whites took shape around those experiences, and what got hold of me was believing that you had to be careful around assholes like that—watch what you say and do and never give too much of yourself away. It wasn't about them being smarter or quicker or more on top of their game than blacks, because that just didn't prove out. It was just the opposite. They seemed like they didn't even know what the game was, much less how to play it or what it took to win. When you get everything handed to you on a silver platter, you lose your edge, and I came to understand that anyone who didn't know what was going on under their noses could do you damage just by getting you caught up in their blind bullshit. It's important to trust the individuals you let get close to you. They've got to know what you know. You've got to operate on the same principles.

Some fool who can't keep his own shit together isn't going to be much help in keeping your pimp hand strong. You've got to be stupid to hang around with stupid people, and I'll tell you one thing, free of charge: if I owned a big fine house on the hill full of Game Boys and goat cheese hamburgers and crystal figurines, I sure as shit wouldn't let some little nigger kid from Long Beach have the run of the place without a full cavity search at the end of the day.

Does that make me prejudiced? You call it what you want. I don't hold any rich white dude to blame when he sees me and my homies coming down the street and crosses his ass over to the other side. And I don't expect to be held to account for not inviting him over to my crib and introducing him to my little sister. All men may be brothers, like it says in the Bible, but that doesn't mean we've all got to pretend we're one big happy family. White is white and black is black and I figure God must have made us different for a reason. You can learn to live with the difference or you can just keep telling yourself it doesn't matter. One way you can maybe get along. The other way you can maybe get yourself killed.

Word: I'm not saying the races don't have a common human bond. I'm just saying that bond isn't about compassion and equality and tolerance. What we all share together is the drive to get what's ours and keep it for as long as we can. We're all in the same pursuit of happiness, the same race for the best that life has to give, the same search for respect and props and scrilla. We've got the same urges and drives, and those impulses and desires make us ripe to exploit each other. We're either looking for God's direction in our lives or just letting our dicks lead us around. We're either walking down a spiritual path or we're down some blind alley, hoping to get hooked up with our main man.

I'm trying to get straight for you all that it's not necessarily the best in us that brings us together, but the worst. Greed and hatred and every motherfucking criminal impulse that you can think of: that's what blacks and whites—and, for that matter, yellows and browns and reds—have in common. None of us are immune to evil and I wouldn't be making that claim if I hadn't seen it, straight up, with my own eyes.

I'm here to tell the truth, remember? And the truth is, there's no difference I could ever tell between a black whore and a white whore,

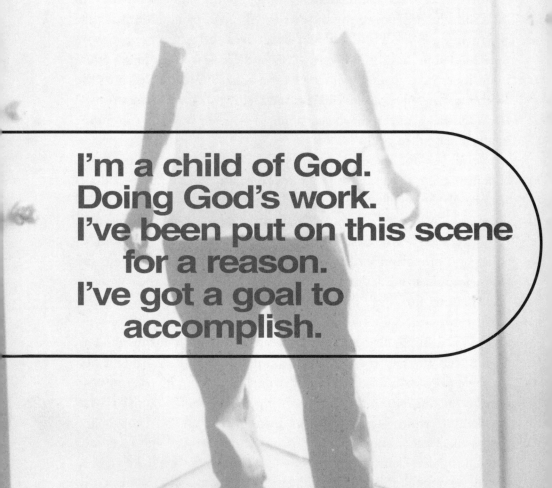

**I'm a child of God.
Doing God's work.
I've been put on this scene
for a reason.
I've got a goal to
accomplish.**

between a black crackhead and a white crackhead, and for that matter, between a black cop and a white cop. We're all dealing with the evil that's inside us and it doesn't do any good to point your finger at someone else and blame them for the dark desires you got lurking in your heart. It's no race thing, or poverty thing, or education thing. It's a human thing. We're all sinners, God says, and I always believe what God tells me. Because He's God.

And even if I was so foolish not to accept Him at His word, I still got all the evidence of my motherfucking senses telling me what's what. It didn't take going clear across town to those big fancy neighborhoods and getting a firsthand look at the lifestyles of the rich and famous to show me that white people have got problems in their lives they just don't want to face up to.

I could see that clear enough when they came down to my side of town, looking to ease the pain and fear and doubt that was eating away at them, the only way they knew how—by blowing it all away in a fat white cloud of crack smoke.

You might say that job I had selling candy on the street was like a training program to get me ready for the next step up the ladder of financial success. Only this time the candy I was selling was bad for a whole lot more than your grille and I didn't have to go out looking for the customers—they come to me, twenty-four seven, three hundred and sixty fucking five, with those big bills clenched in their sweaty hands and their eyes all beady and bright and that rasp in their voice that's about halfway between a whisper and a scream when they're asking you extra nice if you can please hook them up.

Experts are always talking about the economics of selling drugs as if any nigger with a third-grade education couldn't figure out from jump the simplest law of supply and demand: if you got a supply of what everyone demands, that's all the economics you're ever going to need. Naturally, peddling crack or chronic or crank or shine or whatever else is getting folks where they want to get is going to pay you more than flipping fishwiches at McD's or sitting on your ass in a bullet-proof booth at a gas station, taking money through a slot.

And when you got a whole generation up ahead of you trying to support themselves and their families with low-paying and menial jobs, you learn firsthand what it means to be stuck at the bottom of the ladder. And youngbloods aren't stupid, regardless of what their elders are always trying to tell them. They can see straight enough what twelve hours pushing a mop on the night shift will get you up against twelve hours standing on the corner selling dubs to the regulars.

That's where I learned the true nature of black and white, rich and poor, self-esteem and self-destruction. Selling rock is the best way I know to get a good look at human nature on the flip side, down and desperate, with none of the fake bullshit that's supposed to make us civilized. A white man in a Mercedes and a two-thousand-dollar suit is no different than a nigger in a Hyundai and three-day-old sweats when it comes to getting high. They're both ready to do what it takes, pay what it costs, and take any risk just to draw down on that rock one more time.

I've seen them all—five-hundred-dollar-an-hour attorneys and five-dollar-a-night whores; off-duty cops and schoolteachers on their lunch hour; housewives with their kids in the backseat and rock stars in the back of limos; whites and blacks, young and old, rich and poor—nobody is immune from degrading themselves with drugs. And as long as the customers keep coming, the nigger on the corner is going to keep supplying. That's more than supply and demand. That's a pure fact of life.

Experts will tell you that the war on drugs can only be won when we lock up all the dealers, or get tough with all the users, or build a twelve-foot wall between us and the motherfuckers on the other side of the border. I don't know about any of that shit, but I can tell you this, from firsthand experience: this war everyone's supposed to be fighting won't be over until someone invents a cure for getting high. You take away all the cocaine, fools will still be smoking indo; you take away the indo they'll be drinking; you bring back prohibition, they'll start sniffing glue. Let's face it—getting faded is a basic human drive, like food and water and sex and sleep. It's never been about some kind of so-called socioeconomic disadvantage. You can't educate people into staying straight; there's no percentage in trying to scare people away from whatever it is that scratches that particular itch. All you can do is admit that most all of us have got it, that addictive pull, then leave the choice up to each one of us. And whatever each one of us decides is worth living for, that's what we're going to give ourselves over to, heart and soul, mind and body. You can't explain that away, or pass a law against it, or try to convince everybody to *just say no.* For most motherfuckers that's like saying no to air. And there's no one alive that can hold their breath for that long.

chapter seven

Gangsta cool,
Snoop style.

chapter seven

Like I said from the beginning, I'm not going to lie to you. The good, the bad, and everything that comes in between— that's all part of this book, and I'm not going to leave anything out to make myself or someone else look good.

The reason I can speak with such authority about the subject of drugs and the hold they can have on a nigger's life is that I've been there. The actual fact is, I'm still there. I've been smoking chronic since before I can remember and nothing's changed. I'm still blowing up-ward of an ounce a day, between me and my posse. There's hardly a time between when I wake up and when my head hits the pillow that I'm not toking on a blunt, rolling one up, or passing one around.

Marijuana is a fact of my life, and if you don't like it, you can kiss my black ass. An ounce a day is what you might call a major commitment to getting high and staying high, and if you want to call that an addic-tion, I'm not going to argue the point. I depend on indo for all kinds of things—to get my creative flow going in the studio, to help me deal with the high-pressure job of staying one step ahead of the music busi-ness, to keep me calm and cooled out when everyone else around me is watching and wondering what move I'm going to make next. For some fools, it's a three-martini lunch, a bottle of Château Lâfitte at dinner, and a snifter of Hennessey at bedtime. For me, it's a blunt of sinsemilla for breakfast, a blast of bud for lunch, and whatever's left in the ashtray for a late-night snack.

I'm not going to get into all that tired shit about pot being better for you than booze, or whether you're better off smoking a joint or a cigarette. That's what motherfuckers tell themselves when they're trying to justify their habits and vices, and I don't need justification. I am what I am and I do what I do and I don't have to answer to anyone but God. Weed is my escape, and my best guess is if we didn't all need to escape every once in a while, there'd be no one popping Prozac or snorting shine or drinking a six of Colt 45 just to get up for the weekend, when the *serious* partying takes place. I don't care if you're the poorest welfare case in the ghetto or the richest rap star on the charts—everybody's carrying their own cross and we all need to lighten that load when we can.

Sometimes the truth is complicated. And sometimes it's simple. The situation with chronic is definitely one you can't work out on a one-plus-one tip. It just won't add up if you try it that way. On one side of the equation, I've got a lifelong habit, a way of getting through the hard times and celebrating the good times that I'm not so sure I could do without, and I'm damn sure I wouldn't even want to try. On the other side, I've got two young sons who never had the chance to fuck up their lives by learning to depend on something else besides themselves and the gifts God gave them in the first place. I've got to ask myself—would I want them to follow in my path? After all, they wouldn't have any trouble finding it . . . just follow the smell of smoke that dogs me wherever I go.

But do I want them tripping down places they may not be able to find their way out of? Am I setting a good example for my sons? Will the day come when I sit them down, take out a blunt, and teach them how to hold that smoke down deep in their lungs until they feel that rush and start seeing those colors exploding behind their eyeballs?

I don't think so. If it ever gets to the point where my sons ask me about drugs, I'm going to tell them what I truly feel. They're better off without them. I owe them that much, and if that makes me a hypocrite, then that's just a charge I'll have to cop to. The way I look at it, anyone who uses drugs and tells you how bad they can be when they get a hold of your life isn't just some authority figure trying to get you to behave. He knows what he's talking about . . . from experience.

Maybe that experience came too late to keep him clean, but that doesn't make what he's saying a lie. It just means he's got something to teach the youngsters that he can draw out directly from his own failures and shortcomings.

So you best believe I'm going to tell my kids what I've learned from experience when the time comes. But, being my kids, I wouldn't be at all surprised if they went ahead and did just what they wanted to, anyway. Maybe they'll take my advice, and maybe they won't follow my example. But chances are, they'll shine what I tell them and take after what I do. That's the way kids are, they learn by example, and, although I'm careful not to let them see me smoking, they're not stupid. They can figure out what's going on. Kids always do, and when they do, it's going to be up to them to decide which direction to turn. I've got to live my life . . . and, when all's said and done, they've got to live theirs, too.

By the time I reached sixteen and got into the twelfth grade, the life I was leading was starting to catch up with me. I'd made my peace with Mama and she'd let me move back into her place, but even with her guidance, I was walking into situations where I couldn't see around the next corner or what was coming up behind me. Those days when I was just a little kid, watching cartoons, riding my beat-up old BMX, and stealing candy from the corner store, were fading fast from my view. And what was rising up before my eyes was a whole other scene, where nothing was what it seemed to be, there was no place to hide, and my mama couldn't take me in her arms and kiss away all the pain and confusion.

After that summer selling candy with G, I went back to school like I'd always done, ready for another year of teachers, homework, and hall monitors, but this time without that innocent assurance that the grown-ups knew what was best and it was up to us youngsters to earn their approval and follow the rules. I guess it comes to every kid sooner or later—that sneaking suspicion that your elders don't know what's up any better than you do, that what they're telling you is just a lie to keep you in line, and that if they were so smart, what were they doing stuck in these dead-end jobs, with no money, no future, and no props?

That's one way of looking at it—a youngblood's way, and you can't really blame them for wondering if there's something better they can reach for than what their parents and teachers are dangling in front of them.

I was no different. By the time I reached sixteen, I thought I knew the game cold, and there wasn't anyone going to tell me any different. I was full of shit, of course, but at sixteen that just comes with the territory. If the truth be told, I wasn't all that sure of myself as I pretended to be, and like I said, that comes with the territory, too. I wanted to be a bad motherfucker and run with the big boys; I just didn't know how to get in the race. So I ended up with one foot in the real world and the other back in my childhood, trying to get enough balls to make the jump and looking over my shoulder the whole time, halfway wishing I could just take a step back and enjoy life like it used to be, when things were simple and innocent and all brand new.

But things weren't simple, not any more, and by 1987, there wasn't anything innocent about the 'hood. As far as school went, it was the same old shit, nothing new there and nothing to keep me involved in getting an education. Whatever I needed to learn I could pick up on the street; that's the way I had it figured, and in a way, it was true. The ghetto had turned, day by day, into a more dark and dangerous place to live. If you didn't know your way around, there was a good chance you wouldn't survive in those conditions, and all the algebra and geography and wood shop in the world wasn't going to help your situation.

I'm not saying education isn't important. I'm just saying there's different kinds of learning. What you find out in books is one kind of knowledge. What you find out on the streets is another. And the knowledge it takes to put them together is probably the most valuable lesson you're ever going to learn. The problem is, they don't teach a class in that. At least, not in any class I ever attended.

And the ones I did attend, during those first weeks and months of my senior year, sounded like the same old bullshit I'd been hearing all through high school. This is what they had promised us was going to be our best year, when we'd be top dog on campus and get to graduate with a cap and gown and a diploma you could frame and put up on your wall and a yearbook full of memories that would last a lifetime.

Instead, it felt like we were all inmates in a maximum-security pen, where everybody was locked down tight and just waiting for some signal to tear the roof off the motherfucker. The late eighties were not what you'd call the best of times in the 'hood—the gangs and the crack and the drive-bys brought down the cops, riding your ass for no other reason than that they were scared, too, and looking over their shoulder for someone to pop a cap from an alleyway or out the window of a car. A plan for the future meant figuring out how to get through one day to the next, and career counseling was about trying to get yourself some protection by hooking up with the Crips or the Bloods. We were living in a war zone and the front lines ran right through the high school classrooms.

It was only a matter of time before I got caught up in that war. After school started, I found myself a job as a box boy at the Lucky's down on Long Beach Boulevard to earn a little pocket change and help my mama out with the groceries and utilities. It was what they call an "entry-level position" without ever telling you that there isn't *but* one level. Which was fine by me. The last thing I wanted to do was work my way up to assistant manager or cashier with one of those name tags telling everyone you're celebrating twenty years on the job, or that nigger with the nozzle watering down the produce. None of that was my idea of opportunity knocking, and bagging people's TV dinners was about as far as I wanted to go in the supermarket game.

The fact is, I was so far down the ladder I'd have to step up to get under, and no one was fooling anyone else by promising the box boy making a hundred and fifty a week before taxes that he had a future with the Lucky corporation. I would have quit after the first week if it hadn't been for the look of pride on my mama's face when I brought home my first paycheck. I may have already had one foot out the front door, but it was still important to me to make her happy and give her something to brag on, and if that little bullshit job did the trick, then I figured I'd stick with it until something better came along.

That something better was a choice that every youngblood in the ghetto has to face sooner or later, and the direction he chooses is going to make a difference for the rest of his life . . . whether he knows it or not. The stakes are high, but there's no way to know that when you're trying to figure out what's what and what your main move ought to be.

Word: if someone asked *you* to pick what was behind Curtain A and Curtain B you might have a hard time deciding where the new car and the bedroom set and the Acapulco vacation was hidden. But if someone opened up those curtains and showed you where the big prize was, sitting there waiting for you, you'd have to be a fool not to grab it and get out before someone changed his mind.

So let me put it to you: behind Curtain A you got a hundred-and-fifty dollar-a week job, working nine to five with overtime (that is, whenever the boss feels like laying it on), maybe a week's vacation, maybe not, and some kind of bullshit benefits that you're going to collect on when you're old and sick and too worn out to spend the cash. You're wearing some uniform that makes you feel like a circus clown, you've got to take a lot of disrepect from people you've never seen before and might never see again. Except every day you looking at the same tired faces, telling the same tired stories, and talking the same tired trash.

But behind Curtain B, you're pulling down maybe *fifteen* hundred dollars a week, maybe more, and doing nothing much besides hanging on the corner with the coolest homies in the 'hood, playing a beat box and polishing your flow, and everyone that comes along to buy your wares is happy to see you and is sure to treat you with all the props you deserve. You don't have to wait for Friday night to roll around to party down with your best clients and all the fine bitches that want to be around you because of what you're carrying in your pocket. A Tuesday is as good as a Saturday; every night is an opportunity to get down and loud until the sun cracks over the horizon and you head back to your plush crib to crash for a few hours, then get up and start all over again.

Don't forget, you're sixteen years old and you've been staring at all the best that the world has to offer—big cars and flashy threads and aftershave that make you dizzy with the smell of success—flashed into your funky, broke-down housing-project bedroom twenty-four seven over the TV. All you know for sure is you want a taste of that so bad it's like a burning down in the pit of your stomach. So, what's it going to be, contestant: Curtain A or Curtain B? You can work at Lucky's or you can get lucky. It's all up to you.

Like I was saying, experts are always talking about the economics of selling drugs in the ghetto and how the government's got to make it worth your while to do something else with your life—be a service to the community and instill a sense of self-worth and all that bullshit. But I'm here to tell you the truth—even if they were paying you two hundred dollars an hour to be a box boy at the supermarket, they're still going to have a problem when it comes down to young niggers making that fundamental choice. Making money is the bomb, don't get me wrong. But there's another reason youngsters are turning to the gangsta lifestyle. It's cool, fool.

Am I telling you something you don't know? Then, straight up, you *are* a fool, and a bigger one than I thought. You've been believing what they've been feeding you in school in those civics class and D.A.R.E. assemblies, about being responsible and making a difference in the community, but the one fact they left out is the one that makes the biggest difference of all. Niggers are running the gangsta game because it's the *image* that appeals to them. No one's out there thinking about the *consequences* of their *actions*. Nobody is interested in what drugs and guns and gangs are doing to the community. Shit . . . drugs and guns and gangs *is* the community, the only community most niggers are ever going to be a part of. And until you can give them something better to belong to—and I'm not talking about midnight basketball or summer jobs or junior fucking achievers—they're going to be shooting at each other and selling drugs to each other and getting each other pregnant and all that other shit that makes respectable citizens wring their hands and stroke their chins and ask themselves where they've gone wrong.

Gangs are cool.

Drug dealers are cool.

Pimps and players are cool.

You think I'm down with that, that I want those motherfuckers to be the role models for my kids? No way. But I'm trying to tell the truth here, and the truth is, we've got a image problem in the ghetto. It's a whole underworld way of life that gives youngsters more to live for, more to believe in, than anything they're hearing in school, in church, or around the dinner table. Shit, we got too many kids too stoned to learn anything in school, too tired to get their asses to church, and too poor to have a dinner table with any fucking food on it. *That's* the reality, and anyone's going tell them how they should be living their lives, they better make sure they've got those facts well in hand.

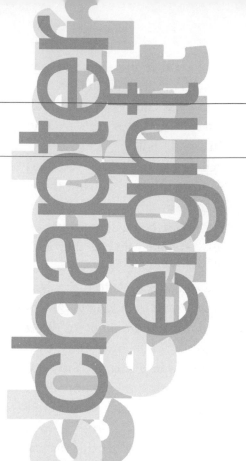

chapter eight

Chillin' out before a show.

chapter eight

For me, sixteen years of age was the turning point. I was too old to be a youngblood anymore, and too young to be able to take charge of my game. Niggers noticed me, and it's no wonder. I'd sprouted up almost overnight and was topping out over six feet by the time I started my senior year. There was no way I could stay under the radar with that kind of size on me. I got asked a lot if I was going to get serious about sports, especially basketball, and, although I still loved the game, I definitely had other things on my mind right about then.

Somewhere around that time, it was as if a switch inside of me got turned off . . . or maybe on. What mattered before didn't seem to make much difference anymore. I still loved my mama and wanted to do whatever it was that would make her happy, but I didn't want it bad enough to stay clear of the things that I knew made her sad and scared and protective of me. She knew I was blowing a lot of chronic—I'd actually started getting regular with it about a year before—and she asked me, sometimes even *begged* me, to stop. It didn't make any difference that the nigger who had lit my first blunt was her own brother. She and I both knew that if it hadn't been Marvin, it would have been someone else, but now that I'd been turned out, so to speak, she had to act out her part as the mama—the one who did what she could to keep me off the wrong track. And, of course, I had to play out my role, right alongside of her—the teenage rebel with a chip on his shoulder and a case to prove. It wasn't like anything changed between us, deep down inside. It was more like I had to make my own way and the only way I could do that was to let her know I wasn't under her control anymore. That's just what growing up is all about. No one ever said it was going to be easy.

I was heading for trouble, and Mama made sure I knew it. What I couldn't explain to her was that I was *looking* for trouble. I wanted to shake up my life, the routine that had worn into a dull groove during my childhood and was making me feel like nothing was ever going to change. Hell, I was no different from any other sixteen-year-old on this planet. I wanted some action, some excitement, some thrills, chills, romance, and adventure. I wanted my life to be like one of those action movie previews we saw down at the multiplex—all the highlights singled out and strung together so you can hardly catch your breath between the explosions, the car chases, and the beautiful bitches ready to bump.

But I don't have to tell you that most of those movies turn out to be a rip-off, anyway. Between all the good parts is the boring shit that they never show you in the coming attractions. It isn't until you've already paid for your ticket and sat down with your jumbo tub of popcorn and extra-large Coke that you realize they played you for a sucker. It's never as good as they tell you it's going to be.

Dig where I'm heading with this? Most of the shit that people try to sell you never comes across as advertised. The name of the game is to get you to believe the hype. Then the rest is easy. When you sell yourself on something, you're committed to what you buy because nobody wants to look like a fool and admit they've been played. You're just another link in the chain that stretches from generation to generation and keeps us all enslaved.

Look at the so-called gangsta lifestyle. The brothers in Long Beach are no different than the 'bloods in any other ghetto across this country—they're looking to believe and to belong and build themselves up into something bigger than they really are. That's what gangs are selling and that's what the niggers are buying, and just like peddling dope, what you've got here is a perfect example of supply and demand. Gangs are in business because youngbloods need to belong to something, and if the community can't find a place for them, there'll always be more than enough room in a continuing criminal enterprise.

That's the legal term, a continuing criminal enterprise: an organization created and operated for illegal gain. A racket. A mob. And where I come from you can take your choice of competing corporations—Crips or Bloods. Six of one or a half dozen of another. There ain't no difference. It's all about which color you want to wear, which homeboys you want to hang with, which pledge of allegiance you want to stand up and salute. And in the end, you really can't tell one from the other.

Of course, my partiality was always toward the Crips. To me, those niggers had a history, a tradition that held them together and gave them something to be proud of. But that was just the way I put it together. I'm sure any self-respecting Blood could tell you why his gang's the bomb and the Crips ain't shit. I'm not here to argue the point. All I'm trying to do is shed a little light on the situation and try and explain how come it is that we've got ourselves a full-scale urban war going on all around us.

Black gang history in L.A. goes back clear back to the 1920s, with crews like the Goodlows, the Boozies, and the Magnificents. Back in the day, it wasn't about hardcore crime as much as just having an identity that could set you apart from all the other poor niggers out from Mississippi and Chicago or wherever else, looking for a piece of Cali sunshine. By the fifties, you had your basic car clubs—the Businessmen, the Slausons, the Gladiators—brothers who basically ruled South Central and the 'hoods of East L.A.

It was after the Watts riots that the situation started to get out of hand. Gangs were getting militant and, since they couldn't attack the white power structure, they turned on each other—with bats and chains and all the kinds of primitive weapons that poor people use to express their rage and helplessness.

Right around that time, a nigger from out in Compton named Raymond Washington—along with his main man Stanley Williams, a.k.a. Tookie—started a crew called the Baby Avenues, as a sort of spin-off from an older gang called the Avenue Boys. Legend has it that Washington changed the gang's name to the Avenue Cribs to go along with the whole "baby" tip. Then one night when they were out knocking off a corner grocery store owned by a Korean, the cops showed up and the Cribs took off running down the block, followed by the clerk who was yelling in his bad English, *"Crips! Crips!"* A white reporter who was on the scene wrote up the story for the newspapers the next day, using the name he'd heard the Korean dude shouting. The Crips were born.

Before long the gang had grown in size and reputation, swallowing up all kinds of smaller crews in and around the L.A. 'hoods. By the mid-seventies, there were the Eastside Crips and the Westside Crips; the Compton Crips and the Avalon Garden Crips; the Inglewood Crips and the Piru Street Crips.

The fact is, the Bloods themselves were formed out of a Crips gang that had splintered off the main organization after they'd lost a street fight with the Compton crew. The breakaway gang got some other, smaller crews to throw in with them, changed their colors from a blue rag to a red rag, and the Bloods were on their way to becoming the Crips' biggest rivals in the region, even though they were outnumbered three to one.

From jump, the Crips had the reputation to go with their size. Down in Long Beach we had a Crip chapter for every 'hood in the city and they were known from north to south, east to west, as some of the meanest and most ruthless gangs around. Even today, you ask any brother on the street what his worst nightmare would be, it'll more than likely have the Seven Day or West Coast Crips mixed in it somewhere. And if the nigger really knows his shit, he'll mention the Insane Crips Gang—only he won't say it too loud, in case someone should hear him and think he was talking trash about those vicious motherfuckers. The ICG would as soon cut you wide open as look at you and nobody, but nobody had the balls to fuck with them. They were rabid dogs set loose on the neighborhood, and I still get a cold chill sometimes thinking about them.

I never had the nerve to get too close to the ICG. My gang was the Twenties, the Rolling 20 Crips from down out along Twentieth Street. Even though a lot of my homies, including cousins and uncles and such, were riding with the ICG, I had more respect for myself than to push my luck that far. Hanging with the ICG could get you killed

when you were looking the other way, and all I was after was to get my scrilla in shape. I needed cash to support myself in the style I wanted to become accustomed to and that, short and sweet, was what the Twenties were all about.

Don't get me wrong. We had our share of riders, gangstas, thugs, hustlers, ballers, and killers. It's just that, when I got put on, the main emphasis at that time was purely cash. We liked money and we liked what we could get with money and we weren't too especially particular where we got the money to get what we wanted. We were straight up capitalists and we had a very simple theory of economic determination: we were about the green. Crime, for us, wasn't an end unto itself, it was a means to an end. Robbery, dealing, burglary, jacking car stereos, snatching purses, and shoplifting athletic shoes . . . that was all just about getting paid. Other niggers might steal and rob and kill for the thrill of it. The Twenties got our thrill from a big choking wad of dead presidents in our pockets.

The media is always talking trash about gang initiations, like the brothers were trying to keep the whole thing exclusive or something. There's even one urban myth that's still alive about how, before you can wear colors, you got to drive around at night with your headlights off. You're supposed to cap the first dude in a passing car that flashes you to turn them on, and that gets you in. Which is the biggest bunch of bullshit I ever heard—just white paranoia run wild.

Word: getting put on is about the easiest thing in the world. At least it was for me. I knew a nigger named Blue who'd been with the Rolling Twenties since I was in grade school and, when the time came for me to make my move, I just walked up to him in broad daylight right on Long Beach Boulevard and told him I wanted in. There was nothing secret or special about it and it's about as hard to do as getting a Blockbuster video card or joining the Vons Club. Shit, they *want* you in. There's strength in numbers, and at the time I hooked up with the Twenties, there were well over two hundred brothers wearing our colors.

Of course, there were certain formalities. They picked out a couple of hulking niggers and put me up to spar with them for a couple of rounds, but it was more for fun than anything else. We all made sure not to be punching too hard and after it was over we all partied down at Blue's crib.

I couldn't tell you for sure that joining the Twenties made me feel a whole lot different—I didn't stand too much taller or walk and talk with a new attitude. It was more like buying a life-insurance policy. You maybe don't need it right away, but it's good to know you got it in reserve, just in case you've got to deal with a situation that you can't handle on your own. Most of the homies in the Twenties had been around the 'hood for years anyway. I'd known them and hung with them and even pulled off some petty shit with them on occasion. It was more or less business as usual, except for what you might call my new corporate identity.

The Twenties represented what I was about at that time—living large and throwing down major scrilla. To me, it was like making an investment in the future. The Crips could help me get where I wanted to go, and if that meant they had a claim on my life . . . well, that didn't seem too big a price to pay.

But looking back now, I'd have to say that joining a gang was like crossing some invisible line, and once I was on the other side, there was no turning back. Life may have gone on with its usual routine, but when I looked at myself in the mirror, I was seeing a different image. I was a *Crip* and I was suddenly carrying around everything that came with that name. In the Bible it talks about the mark of Cain, like the brother had a tattoo or something on his forehead that set him apart and made people look the other way when he walked by. In the same way, it was like I had the mark of Crip on me, a symbol that I was part of something bigger than myself, something that gave you authority and power . . . and instilled fear.

I was proud of that identity, but at the same time I didn't know if I could totally commit myself to living up to the motherfucking myth of a bad-ass gangsta. It was like wearing threads that were too big for you and when you try to fill them out, you hope no one notices that the shoulders don't fit and the cuffs are dragging on the sidewalk. I think that maybe it was just the last remnants of being a kid that made me feel awkward. Joining the Crips was like telling yourself and everyone else that you'd become a man—whether or not you really felt like one.

And, since I was a man, it was high time I took my place in a man's world. If going to school seemed like a waste of time *before* I was put on the Twenties, that was nothing compared to how it looked to me after I started wearing colors. Nothing they were trying to teach me in school was ever going to make a bit of difference to the world I had just stepped into. It was time to get out and get on with it.

While I couldn't tell you that I planned the whole thing out in advance, I knew going in what the outcome would have to be. And that was the whole idea. If they were going to cut me loose, I'd have to give them a good reason, which is exactly what I did one morning not long before graduation when I showed up in homeroom with the biggest, fattest blunt I could roll hanging out of the corner of my mouth. I stepped down the aisle—with kids staring after me, laughing and rolling their eyes and giving each other high fives like I was some kind of outlaw hero come to set their asses free—and sat down at my desk letting out the smoke from a big toke and tipping the ash onto the floor. The teacher came charging over to me and I held up the joint like maybe she wanted a pull and the whole class took to yelling and cheering and carrying on while the teacher got on the intercom and called for security.

I was out before lunch, with a note to take to my mama. But I didn't go home, at least not right away. Instead I took a stroll down Long Beach Boulevard, enjoying my newfound freedom and finishing off that blunt. I ran across a couple of older brothers from the Twenties and told them what I'd done and was proud of myself all over again to see the look of respect on their faces.

We spent the rest of the morning down at King Park, just kicking back and watching the world go by. I didn't have anywhere else to be until five that afternoon, when I had to show up for my job at Lucky's, and by the time the afternoon finally rolled around, I'd decided to finish off the job I'd started that morning and make a clean break from anything else that was tying me down. When I finally showed up at work I was an hour late and was completely faded on the fine indo some of those homies had been holding back for a special occasion. When I kicked it through the automatic doors, swaying in time to some tune that was playing in my skull, I didn't even have to bother to submit my resignation. The manager took one look at me and pointed my ass back out onto the sidewalk.

My new friends were waiting for me out there, including Blue, who took me back to his crib for some more celebrating, and I didn't get out of there until the sun had gone down and the street had emptied out from the rush-hour traffic. Needless to say, I was feeling no pain as I walked down the block just as the streetlights came on, one after another down along the whole length of the boulevard like those blue lamps you see along an airport runway, guiding jets to a safe landing back home.

But there wasn't going to be a safe landing for Snoop Dogg Airlines, and no home to come back to. I'd turned away from all that, and looking back on it now, I'd have to say I was throwing it away without so much as a second thought. When you're sixteen you don't have a whole lot of practice thinking things through, and, anyway, I'd been so high all day long that I truly don't believe it actually occurred to me that I'd come face-to-face with my mama until I turned the corner to our street and saw the lamp in our apartment window shining like beacon.

It was then I realized that she'd be there, waiting for me, wondering what happened to her little baby boy, and I suddenly didn't feel so much like a man anymore. In fact, right then, I think I would have given anything to go back to the way it was, when I'd open up the front door, drop my books on the table, and set myself down in front of the TV to watch some cartoons while, from the kitchen, I could smell Mama cooking dinner and hear her playing one of her favorite old soul records, singing along to keep herself company.

But those days were gone, and as I stopped in the street and stared up at the light in the window, I knew way down in the pit of my stomach that they weren't coming back. They say that grown men don't cry, and I guess that's how I knew that night that I hadn't quite made it to manhood.

chapter nineteen

Snoop Dogg, well marinated.

chapter nine

've got to hand it to Moms, though. She didn't throw me out on my ass that first night I came home with no job and a suspension notice from school. She'd have been well within her rights to do it, and I wouldn't have put up a fight. After all, I'd thrown all her love and care and concern right back in her face. By what I did, I'd as good as told her I didn't give a fuck what she thought or how she wanted to raise me up. I was going to do exactly what I wanted and if that didn't go right with her, she could mind her own damn business.

The only thing Mama asked me that night was to please go back to school and see if they would let me graduate. After all, I only had a week or so left and it was a shame to have gone through all those years and not have a diploma to show for it. I hated to admit that she was right, but the next morning I did what she asked and got permission from the principal to graduate while they were sorting out my situation. The fact was, my grades were good and I was right up there in the top third of my class. Graduation wasn't ever going to be a problem for me until I made it one.

Looking back, of course, I'd have to say it was one of the best decisions I'd ever made and, to this day, I'm proud that I got through high school in spite of all the shit that I pulled. I thought I knew what was what, and no one could tell me different, and because of that ignorant attitude, I almost lost out on a milestone in my life.

But here's the twist—it was my mama in the first place who taught me about being independent, about doing things my own way no matter what anybody else had to say about it. It was a lesson she taught by example, like when she threw her worthless boyfriends out of the house, even though she knew she'd have to go back to living on her own and trying to raise a family by herself. My mama never took shit from anyone and she made sure I had the same point of view, boosting my belief in myself and giving me the self-confidence to take things on, even when the odds were against me.

I guess she never figured I'd use her own techniques against her, but my understanding is that it's always that way between parents and youngsters. They're looking to pass on the values and knowledge that it's going to take for you to get by in this world, and first thing you do with all that self-assurance is to tell them you don't need their love and protection anymore, that you handle it yourself from here on out. I did it to my mama and I'm betting my kids are going to do it to me.

Of course, looking at it from her side, I can't blame her for all the screaming and crying and throwing things she did that night. Just because she'd taught me to be independent and think for myself, it didn't mean she was going to get behind me when I made a stupid move, and as far as she was concerned, smoking a blunt in class was about as dumb-ass a move as I ever busted. But after all the smoke cleared, so to speak, and she dried her eyes and swept up the broken plates off the kitchen floor, it was clear enough that I still had a place in her home, and when I went to bed that night it felt like I'd had a last-minute reprieve from all the life-changing shit I'd brought down on myself.

But it wasn't going to be too long before I would realize that I'd gone too far down the road to turn back now. The day after graduation, in fact, a pounding on the door pulled me up off my pillow with a jerk, and the next minute a couple of cops in uniform pushed into my bedroom and told me to get dressed. My mama was right behind them, cursing them like she'd cursed me the week before, shouting to keep their big ugly hands off her baby and get out of her house or show her a search warrant.

The fact was, my mama has seen one too many cop shows on TV. These officers didn't need a search warrant to come and bust my ass for smoking marijuana on the grounds of a public school. They were in search of a fugitive from justice, and once they found me, they weren't wasting time with the formalities. While I was still buckling my belt they hauled me out of the apartment and down the stairs with all the neighbors peeking out and the little kids on the sidewalk stopping their games to watch the dangerous criminal brought down like a mad dog.

At least it seemed that way to me. Looking back, I'm guessing those cops were probably bored already with having to waste their morning bringing in some skinny-ass chronic-smoking nigger who was too crazy to know where to light a blunt. This was just business as usual, another day in the Long Beach ghetto, and it wasn't helping their mood to have some bitch running up alongside them screaming about "her baby," and "little Snoop" and all that. The whole scene was like a dream to me at that moment, and that's not because I couldn't believe it was happening. I knew only too well that I had it coming to me. It was just that I couldn't get over the feeling that Mama was carrying on like that just for *my* benefit, that she wanted me to know that she was looking after her baby boy, but at the same time wasn't all that beside herself with sorrow that I was being taken away and taught a lesson.

I spent the next couple of weeks in juvenile detention, waiting for my case to come around and knowing the whole time that the beef was bullshit. They weren't about to waste a perfectly good jail cell on me when they had real-life dealers and murderers and rapists loose on the street with no place to put them. This was all about that "scared straight" routine they always try to run on first-time offenders, hoping that if they make jail seem bad enough, they'll keep you from coming back again.

No chance. First of all, any nigger who's been there—and that's a *lot* of niggers—will tell you that there isn't all that much difference between being inside and outside when it comes to feeling that you're still being denied your basic liberties, as an American and as a plain human being. What I'm trying to tell you is that the joint is like the ghetto, a place where you are caged in and kept an eye on and never left alone long enough to think about where you are and how to get out. Chances are, most of the brothers on your block are homies you knew on the street, and out on the street, most of the homies you hang with are brothers you knew on the block. It's a vicious circle, a revolving door, and after a while the line between being *in* and *out* gets real blurry and all you know for sure is that you're serving time, one way or the other.

But it takes time to get to that place where you're coming up with the attitude that it doesn't really matter if the bars on the window are keeping you in or keeping some other motherfucker out. And before you get there, you've got a chance to turn things around, to make decisions that will free your mind no matter where they throw your body, that will take you out of your sorry victim status and give you the skills to call on your own destiny and make your life work for you.

Anything you do that keeps you from taking that decision, from turning to God and calling on Him for help, is nothing but a waste of time, and I'm telling you the painful truth when I say I wasted a lot of time in jail before I decided to get free of the chains that held me down.

Meanwhile, I just had to suffer, like every other poor sucker who gets ground up in the wheels of American justice. The first time I was locked up wasn't the last time, and even if I knew then what I know now I can't promise you things would be a whole lot different. Being black in this country means serving time, one way or the other, and that's a sad fact. But along with incarceration comes education, the cold truth staring you in face, telling you that a nigger has got the deck stacked against him before he ever starts to play the game, and if you want to win—if you ever want to walk out of those prison gates and never look back—you've got to be smarter, more together and on top of yourself than any white asshole would in the exact same situation. That's called turning your disadvantages in your favor, and jail is the best way I know to change a bad situation into an opportunity.

Jail is like everything you imagine it's going to be, and like nothing you ever expected. It's loud and bright and never shuts down enough to where you can remember what it's like to be alone, but it's also the loneliest place in the world. You got iron cages and lockdowns and guards with gats and fences topped off with razor wire, but you never get the feeling that you're safe and secure. The food will rot out your guts, the air is stale and full of smoke, and the beds feel like they've been stuffed full of gravel, but if you're in there long enough, it gets to feeling like home.

The joint is where the underbelly of the American dream is laid wide open, where all the poverty and racism and crime is distilled down to its purest form. And for that reason alone, when you finally get there it seems familiar in a strange kind of way. It's like waking up in a place where all the bullshit has been stripped away, where a man is free to act out of his true nature and express what's really in his heart and soul. Remember I was saying that black and white are the same not because we're all deep down good, but because we're all deep down bad? Well, in prison is where the deep down gets let loose. You might think a place like that would be hell on earth, but the truth is, it's all around us anyway. We're just all pretending to look the other way. But when you're behind bars, there *is* no other place to look. It's staring you right in the face.

It's no surprise to me that most of the hip-hop and gangsta rap lifestyle is taken directly from the penal system. The baggy clothes and do-rags, the language and the attitude, even the way niggers, and all the little white suburban kids that copy our every move, walk down the street, is all about the daily routine on the block. Word to your mother: even if you don't know it, you'll be acting like a convict, because being a convict in this society is a mark of legitimacy you can't get anywhere else.

To say that I was surprised to find myself locked up would be a lie. Looking back, all I can say is that it was a surprise they didn't throw my ass in jail a lot earlier. But to say that I found a place for myself behind bars would be a lie, too. For better or worse, I wasn't like those other niggers who were serving their time re-creating the world of the streets for themselves. I knew I could get by if I had to, but I also knew that as soon as I got to feeling comfortable in the place, I'd be played for good. Something held me back, some kind of self-preservation that wouldn't let me take that road to becoming a con whether I was in the joint or out on parole.

It's a lesson you learn by looking around you at all those worn-out, toothless, nicotine-stained motherfuckers who've spent more time serving time than they have being free and who don't know any other way to live. I'm not saying those old cons don't have a lot of wisdom to pass along. They decide to take you under their wing and that can make the difference between life and death. They know how to work the system—shit, they *are* the system, regardless of what the guards and the trustees think. They know what's going down at any given minute on any given block in the whole place, and it's the grapevine they got between themselves that keeps the place wired and the brothers from getting crazy with the boredom and solitude and day-in-day-out hassles you've got to deal with when you're living in a cage.

But the best lesson those old-school cons can teach a youngster is the one they show you by example. You see them in their cells at night after lockdown or in the morning before roll call, laying on their bunks with all pictures they cut out of magazines stuck up around them on the walls. And they'll be reading some worn-out paperback, or listening to some tired oldies station, or just staring up at the steel ceiling like they've been doing every day, year in and year out for their whole damn lives and it doesn't take a lot to see yourself in there, rotting away from the inside until they haul your sorry carcass away and replace it with another one that's going to sit in that cell and stare at that ceiling until . . . well, you get the idea.

Of course, the first time they put me away, in juvenile detention, I didn't have those old-timers around to show me what I was facing. We were a bunch of wild youngbloods, hollering and sparring and trying our best to show everyone we were the meanest motherfuckers in the place and no one had better mess with us. But it wouldn't be too much longer before I was on a first-name basis with some of the longest-serving inmates in the system, and I'll always be thankful to those dudes for showing me where I was heading and how I could have thrown my whole life away. I couldn't say turning away one young nigger from a life behind bars justified their existence . . . but maybe it helped, just a little.

Just like I figured I would, I got off with a suspended sentence and probation and was back on the streets before the month was out. I couldn't help but notice that the homies in the Rolling Twenties gave me a new kind of respect when I showed up in the 'hood that afternoon and it was then that I realized that getting popped was the *real* initiation to get into a gang. You weren't really legit in their eyes until you'd been fingerprinted and photographed and given a number. That's what made you a citizen of the streets.

And over the next couple of months I did everything I could to earn my rank in the gang. Once I'd turned the corner, it was like I

Truth comes in many disguises, even a skinny nigger with braids from the east side of Long Beach, California.

just started rolling faster and faster and the more speed I picked up the more blurry things got passing by until it seemed like my life was just one long petty crime spree. It got so that the stealing cars and snatching purses, breaking and entering and shoplifting was a job in itself. I'd have to get up early in the morning and go bed late at night just so I could keep up with all the shit the Twenties had going on. Nobody had to talk me into it and there wasn't some crime boss calling the shots. That's all Hollywood bullshit. Me and the homies would just naturally congregate down at the corner of Twentieth and Long Beach Boulevard, or over by King Park, smoke some weed and drink a few beers until, like they always say, one thing would lead to another and we'd find ourselves running down some alley with an old lady's purse and hiding behind some garbage cans to split thirty-six dollars eight ways or some other sorry-ass bullshit that, in the end, always seemed like a whole lot more trouble than it was worth.

Crime doesn't pay, as the old saying goes, and they got that right. For all the effort we put into ripping off folks' welfare payments, or breaking into a housing-project apartment to lift someone's VCR, we weren't even making a living wage. The fact is, I think I was doing better at Lucky's . . . and I'm damn sure I was working better hours.

And when I wasn't out on the street planning some caper, I'd have to be at home listening to Mama bitch and moan about how I was the shame of her life and bringing dishonor to the family name and anything else she could think of to humiliate me into getting legal work. None of it worked, although she was definitely wearing my patience thin, and I took more and more to hanging with the crew in the Twenties, crashing in their living rooms or just staying out all night and waiting until Mama went to work until I sneaked back home to grab a few hours with the pillow over my head to keep out the sunlight.

This shit couldn't go on for too much longer. The Twenties were supposed to be about the cash, but so far it looked to me like we were scraping the bottom of the barrel when it came to making ends meet. I was going to have to cultivate some new criminal alliances. And I knew just where to go.

It was an afternoon in early fall when I set out looking for a homey

I'd known for years around the 'hood who'd become one of the main players in the Insane Crip Gang. I found him out by a little vacant lot off Thirty-fourth Street where he and his posse used to hang out and take care of business.

Now the connection between the ICG and the Rolling Twenties had always been close. A lot of us came from the same neighborhoods and, like I said, some of my own relatives were rolling with the Insane. It wasn't about drawing a chalk line on the street with one side belonging to each gang. We kind of mixed and blended and, even through the Insane had a reputation as vicious motherfuckers, they were tighter with the Twenties than any other gang in Long Beach. I'd go so far as to say that you get on the wrong side of a Twenty, you're pretty much going to find yourself on the wrong side of the Insane Crips.

So I didn't have any second thoughts about talking my man into hooking me up with whatever he could throw my way to make a little cash. And it turned out to be my lucky day. At least that's one way of looking at it. The nigger was about to make a move on some new territory. If I wanted in, he could maybe find a place for me on a new crew he was putting together. They were going to call themselves the Six One, named after Sixty-first Street and Atlantic Avenue up in the north end of town. They even had the corner picked to make a move on, a nice busy intersection for doing business.

chapter ten

Yo, G—Snoop is in the house.

chapter ten

hen it came to staking out territory where they could sell crack cocaine, the Insane Crip Gang had a real simple approach. It's called terrorism. They made sure their reputation got around, and none of those niggers would ever bother to deny any of the outrageous rumors you'd hear about the ICG. As far as they were concerned, the nastier, the better, so that when the time came for them to move into some other gang's turf, they let the word on the street do most of the work for them.

They'd play it this way. After they found a spot where the crack business was good, like Sixty-first Street and Atlantic Avenue, they'd put together a crew that would have the backing of the Insane to go in there and set up shop. Then they'd take to disrespecting the set that was there before them, calling out their best fighters and matching them, one on one, with the Insane's meanest heavyweights. They'd tag every bus bench and blank wall in the 'hood with insults about the other gang and their mothers and steal the customers that came around looking for their regular connections by either undercutting the price or just threatening to fuck them up if they didn't get with the new game.

A lot of times, the dissed niggers would try to retaliate and get back their lost territory, but in all the years I was on the street running with the Crips I never heard of anyone taking back what the ICG set aside for themselves. Brothers like to talk big, shake their gats in your face and tell you all sorts of shit about how you're never going to see the light of day again, but if you got weight, no one is going to mess with you, no matter what they say.

And with the Insanes in my corner, you better believe I had weight. The day after the recon squad went down to Six One to scope out the scene, I was on the corner with an Insane brother, moving rock like it was popcorn at a Saturday matinee. The drill went something like this: From our Insane connections we'd usually get ourselves fronted about three ounces of good-quality rock for about eighteen hundred dollars an ounce. From each ounce we could most times turn a seven-hundred-dollar profit, maybe more depending on the street supply that week. I can't remember a time when it wasn't strictly a seller's market, but there was still a lot of play in the going rate and you needed to stay competitive if you wanted to keep the customers coming back. Truth was, if you weren't selling it to them, there was always some other nigger who would, and rock cocaine is first and foremost a volume business. You got to move the shit and keep it moving, otherwise you get your inventory backed up and your suppliers won't carry you for very long, since what they're about is a return on their investment.

So you take your ounces and you cut them for retail sale. The usual breakout was twenty little rocks to a vial, called a dub rock or a twenty piece, that sold for twenty-five dollars. With a good count you could usually turn about a hundred dub rock packages from one ounce, which made the transaction worth everyone's while. Any less, you're wasting your time. Any more, niggers start getting greedy. Dealing drugs is about regulation, about keeping the element of surprise down to a minimum and making sure everyone knows what they're getting, right up front.

Most players on the street level, which was where I was, didn't like to sell anything less than a dub rock, but I was a hustler from jump, and I didn't mind breaking my ounces down to nickel and dime packages, or bumping them up to Five-O's or even half ounces. Whatever the traffic would bear. My motto was always to give the customer what he wants and you'll never have to worry about the motherfuckers moving off somewhere else. I could never understand why other players, even some of the ones in the Six One, wouldn't do business with the raggedy-ass basehead who couldn't afford a dub rock but were desperate to get off even if it meant blowing their last five-dollar bill. What the hell were we standing around for, if it wasn't to pass that shit around fair and square, regardless of whatever your particular economic disadvantage might happen to be? Shit, I never thought twice about selling two-dollar pieces if I had a customer that strung out . . . and I had plenty.

Eventually I branched into moving a little weed along with my regular crack load, but I could see right away that the percentages weren't nearly as profitable. For one thing, chronic had more bulk. It was harder to hold and a lot harder to get rid of in an emergency. For another thing, I had the very unprofessional habit of drawing down on my own supply. The first thing any self-respecting dealer will tell you is to never get high off your own supply. That's Rule Number One. But I was so partial to good indo—and I never handled anything that wasn't the best—that lots of times I just couldn't help myself, and then I'd have to scramble on the street and work on a smaller margin just to make up the shortfall.

Weed was one thing, but cocaine was an entirely different matter. After the first few times I never touched that shit again, and I wouldn't to this day. There's something about the way it smells, like you were putting some heavy-duty chemical in your body that wasn't ever supposed to be there. And that feeling was proved out by the effect that blow would have on me. All that grinding-teeth-and-sweaty-palms shit wasn't any way I wanted to live, not even for ten minutes, which was just about how long it took to rip through your body and leave you feeling weak and nervous and craving some more. Cocaine is poison, straight up, and if you're looking for what brought life in the ghetto down to a dog-eat-dog level, then you've sure enough got your culprit.

But the sad reality is, once I was out of the dope trade and into the rap game, I swear I couldn't see a whole lot of difference between the way business was done on one side of the legal line or the other. You got your rip-offs and your scams and your players with attitude and you got a product that everybody wants to carry because they *know* there's a market out there for what you got and they're looking for a piece of the action any way they can get it. Niggers lie, steal, rob, and even kill to get into the rap game, and I can't think of a better way to get into training for the music business than to be selling dope on a street corner in broad daylight—unless it would be selling your ass like a whore out the backseat of a car. One way or the other, you got to keep your pimp hand strong, just to survive.

For the first couple of months I was jamming on my new gig, making the quotas I'd set for myself and going out of my way to get to know the customers that seemed to drop by the corner of Sixty-first and Atlantic any hour of the night or day. It got so I put together a whole list of regulars who wouldn't buy from anyone but me, so that if they saw some other nigger at the spot they'd just ride on by and wait it out until I showed up again. I can't say I exactly felt good about having a whole mob of crackheads looking for me every time they wanted to get high, but on the other hand, I understood that's how you do business, by building your clientele.

More to my liking were the bitches that would come along and offer to trade sex for crack. Some of those whores were really fly, and I took advantage of the offer whenever I could grab a few minutes from my spot to do a little bumping in some hallway or down an alley.

The power that crack cocaine has over people—rich and poor, black and white, proud and humble—is like nothing I've ever seen, and when some of that power would rub off on you, well, you'd have to be a fool to let it slide by without taking a little on for yourself. The fact that I wasn't using the shit myself gave me a superior feeling to all those fucking addicts that came looking for me. It was like I was in control of the situation, in control of their money and pussies and whatever they might have that I wanted. I didn't abuse that power as much as some, but I can't say I didn't make use of it a time or two. Or maybe three. That's the way it was, and I was serious when I said I wasn't going to lie, whether it makes me look bad or not.

Once the ICG had set me up and provided me with protection, I could settle back and start getting my scrilla together and it wasn't too very long before I was carrying a fat wad of bills in my hip pocket just like all the other bangers working the 'hood. It felt good, being able to throw down for whatever I wanted, whenever I wanted it, and while I maybe didn't have enough cold cash to buy a Mercedes or some of the

fine gold jewelry the brothers were starting to sport, I still felt like I was pimping with the best of them. Nothing was going to slow me down now.

Well, almost nothing. Remember I was talking about the Insanes and how they were known from one end of the ghetto to the other about not giving a fuck the way it was or the way it was supposed to be? They didn't call them Insane because they pissed in their pants or drooled out of the corner of their mouths or spent their time jacking off in their hats. They were niggers who didn't live by any rules, not even the ones they had laid down themselves.

So when trouble finally came to the Six One crew, it wasn't entirely unexpected that the ICG was stirring it up. It might not make a whole lot of sense that the Insanes would get it into their heads to rip off their own dope spots, but that's what happened. We'd been warned up front about niggers trying to steal our supply or our cash, and even though I'd always prided myself on being good above the shoulders—on being able to think or talk my way out of any situation—I figured I better get myself some protection, just in case. So I traded a couple of dub rocks to a customer for a funky .38 that I kept tucked in my belt and tried to make sure I had my back covered whenever I was taking care of business. Any dealer will tell you that you never carry your money or your merchandise on you when you're at the job. Instead, you hide it away somewhere close by so you can lay hold of it at a moment's notice when you've got a sale. Of course, since everyone on the street knows that, anybody that wants to rip you off just has to follow you to your stash and take you down right then and there.

I'd always figured that some crazy motherfucker from the gang we had pushed off the corner would come around one day and try to take back the Six One. But when the shit went down, it wasn't some gang-banger on a payback tip that made the move. It was some of the old-line Insanes, the respected homies that you know from a distance, by name and by reputation.

One night a whole carload of these bangers showed up, coked out of their skulls and packing some big-time weaponry. By the time we realized what was going on, it was already too late, and, even if we'd had fair warning, there wasn't anything we could have done about it, anyway. The Insanes were out the door and on us before you could swallow hard, and it wouldn't have done any good to draw down on them or threaten to pop a cap on their asses. I mean, these niggers were supposed to be on *our* side!

The only thing we had left to do was to take off running with these big hardcore motherfuckers breathing down our necks, and the only reason we got away was because we knew the byways and back streets of the north end of town a little better than they did by that time and were able to disappear before they caught us up and forced us to hand over our inventory and all our cash receipts.

That Insane crew came back two or three times, but we'd got wise to their game and managed to keep out of their way. The truth is, the whole time I was peddling crack in the Six One I only got ripped off once, and then I only let it happen because I truly thought my life was at stake.

It was one of those steamy, smoggy days in the middle of August, when the asphalt goes soft in the street and the air is so dirty you can't hardly see the tops of the buildings down Lincoln Avenue. I'd been moving rocks all morning, since it seemed that day like all my customers got the urge to get high at the same time. I worked up a pretty good sweat by the time I took a break for some chicken and biscuits down at Popeye's, drinking down a couple of thirty-two-ounce iced teas just to get cool.

I was on track and chilling by the time I got back to my spot, but as soon as I got settled down on my corner I feel myself getting tense all over again. I saw one of the 'hood's most notorious Sherm smokers hanging around with that crazed look that only a real Sherm freak gets in his eyes. For those of you that never heard the term, a Sherm is a Sherman cigarette soaked in embalming fluid, which is about the most evil shit any mad scientist ever invented. Cocaine is a harsh chemical, for sure, but that juice makes rock seem like a 100 percent natural product, straight from Mother Nature. Sherms make you crazy, pure and simple—you don't know where you are or what you're doing, but you got enough muscle and momentum in you to tear the door off a fucking armored car. No shit, I've seen Sherm heads fight off a dozen big paramedics trying to strap the motherfucker down in the back of an ambulance. Word: Sherm heads are bad news and that's all there is to that.

Anyway, from the look of this dude, he'd obviously been toking all day and I knew I was going to have trouble trying to move him off my corner so I could do business. I sidled up as slow and gentle as I could and started rapping with the brother, just passing the time as I tried to scope out exactly how far gone he really was.

He was out there, all right. The nigger could hardly put three words together and his eyes kept bouncing around in their sockets like pinballs against a flipper. After a couple of minutes of listening to his gibberish, I told him I had to get back to work, hoping he'd get the hint and move off. No such luck. The dumb fuck just stood there, staring at me and sweating drops as big as the dub rocks I was trying to sell. I'm not sure if he heard me or, if he did, whether he even understood the English language, so I said it again and I saw something start to dawn on his face, like the answer to a question he'd been asking himself all day.

What went down next happened so fast I hardly had time to take a breath, much less get out of his way before he was bearing down on me with his eyeballs popping out of his head and spit foaming up in the corner of his mouth. Whatever the question was he'd been asking himself, the answer he got made him mad, and anyone from the street will tell you there's nothing more dangerous than a Sherm head with an attitude. He shoved me up against the wall and leaned in close, not so much like he was trying to scare me, but more like he was trying to get a clear fix on where I was. I could feel his hand at my throat, getting tighter each time he took a deep, ragged lungful of air, and I knew this motherfucker could kill me right then, walk away from the scene of the crime, get a good night's sleep, and never remember a thing in the morning.

Somehow I managed to squirm out from under his grip and I backed up slowly, making sure not to take my eyes off him or make any moves that might freak him out. I ducked into the doorway of an apartment building halfway up the block, where the Rolling Twenties had set up a crash pad and clubhouse, and ran up the stairs as fast as I could, slamming the door behind me, locking it, and propping a chair up against the doorknob.

I'd been using the pad as a place to hide my stash and my cash and I scrambled over the spot under the sink where I'd hidden it away. Right at that moment, my homey Warren G came out of the bedroom where he'd been taking a nap in his boxers, to see what all the noise was about. As he started to ask what's up, there was a pounding at the door like a raging bull had charged down the hall and was battering his way in.

G didn't wait for an explanation. He had that street instinct that told him to move his ass as fast and far as possible, and it didn't take him but two giant steps to reach the open window, climb out on the fire escape, and disappear down the alley. That left me to face the psycho Sherm freak alone, and by the time he broke down the door, I'd gotten together my stash, my money, my gat, my watch, and anything else I had that was worth a dime and handed it over to him without a word. At that moment, trading all that shit for another chance to breathe was the best deal I'd ever made.

chapter eleven

Me and a nigger's best
friend.

chapter eleven

all work and no play makes Snoop a dull nigger. That's not exactly how the old saying goes, but it's close enough. Day in and day out I was working my game at Sixty-first, and if the city gave out Chamber of Commerce awards for the hardest-working dope dealer in Long Beach, you better believe I would have had a plaque hanging right over my fireplace.

But, given the nature of the business, I had as much time for playing as I did for moving merchandise. One of the first things I did with my profits was buy myself a car, a '77 Cutlass Supreme four-door I got off one of the homeboys from Compton for three hundred dollars. It didn't drive for shit, and every time you hit the brakes you could hear it squealing like a bitch in heat, but I loved the lines of that car and the way I looked sitting behind the wheel, like something out of *Superfly*. All that was missing was one of those big floppy pimp hats and a fur-lined coat cut tight at the waist.

Actually, by the time I'd been part of the Six One crew for a few months, I was doing a whole lot more than just sitting in that car. Mama had made it clear to me that if I didn't get myself straight and find myself a legit gig, she wasn't going to tolerate me being under her roof anymore. And right about then I was in no mood for ultimatums—after all, I was a big, bad gangbanger, with a fat roll of cash in my

pocket and enough attitude for a half dozen bad-ass homies put together. The last thing I wanted to hear was my mama telling me how I
was tossing my life down the drain. She just didn't understand, I said to
myself. She didn't have a clue about life on the streets these days. Things
were different than when she was coming up. It was a whole new game
with a whole new cast of characters.

I could have told myself that bullshit all day long, and it wouldn't
have made it a single ounce more true. My mama knew what was up,
she was no fool, and if there's one thing you can say about life in the
'hood, it's that the more things change, the more they stay the same.
Sure, we had drive-bys and gang warfare and kids having kids and all
the rest of the sad stories that go with being black and poor these days.
But when it comes down to the basic rules of survival, there wasn't a
thing my generation could have told my mama's generation that they
didn't already know and hadn't already lived through. The only thing
that had changed was that there was just more of the same—more ways
to lose, more ways to fail, more ways to die. The percentages might
have been different, but the game stayed the same.

Mama knew that I had turned down the wrong road and that the
further I rode along that detour, the harder it was going to be for me to
pull a U and head back. The hardcore criminal life is like that—it's a
habit that feeds on itself until you forget that you ever had the choice
of another way of life to live. Maybe my mama couldn't have stopped
me from making the choices I had, but she sure as hell didn't have to
stand by helpless and watch me take the consequences. It was painful
enough knowing I was trading my future for life on a street corner. But
she'd had enough pain in her day not to want to witness someone she
loved go down. It was time for me to leave.

Getting thrown out of the house again, pushed outside the circle of
my family was really just that last step in the walk I'd been taking ever
since I strolled out of my homeroom with a blunt between my teeth. I
had staked my claim to being a man, and no man hid behind his
mama's apron strings. At least that was the bullshit macho code of con-
duct I was determined to live by. Problem was, I wasn't enough of a
man to leave on my own. It had to be on her to make the move, so I
could tell myself that it was her that forced the choice, instead of ad-

mitting that it was me that had given her no choice. That way, I didn't have to face the real obligation that comes with being a man—taking responsibility for your own actions, and answering to your friends and family before you answer to yourself.

Those lessons would come with time and experience, but right about then I wasn't so much concerned about making a stand to be a man as I was to find a bed to lay my head. I had an old, beat-up suitcase, a couple of cardboard boxes I'd taken out of the back of Lucky's, and a paper bag full of socks and underwear, and that was it—the sum total of my worldly possessions, and no place to put it. Not that anyone would have bothered ripping off that pathetic pile of junk—my old kicks, some 45s, a deflated football, and a ColecoVision with a busted joystick—that was about all I had, the last remains of my former life as a youngblood, and the only thing it was worth was what you might call sentimental value.

I could have stayed over at the gang house that the Rolling Twenties kept up across town, but what with all the comings and goings, sleeping there was like trying to set up house on a freeway on-ramp, and to tell the truth, I just wasn't down for that twenty-four seven shit. I needed a place where I could be by myself, cool out when I needed to, and get some solid shut-eye after a hard day on the street and a long night of partying.

So I set myself up in my Cutlass. I know, I can hear you motherfuckers laughing now, just picturing this big gangly nigger folded up like a pocketknife in the backseat of that funky old car, with his smelly kicks and his busted Coleco and a pile of empty Jack in the Box bags piling up on the floor. The fact was, that's exactly how I lived for the first couple of months after my mama threw my ass out, parked in an alley about a half block away from my corner on Sixty-first, using the bathroom of a 76 station down the street to do my business and jamming down to the Twenties club to take a shower every couple of days.

All in all, I must admit, it wasn't a bad way to chill, at least for the time being. There was no one around telling you to clean your room and make your bed—mainly because you didn't *have* a motherfucking room or a bed. There was no need to worry about putting everything back in its place, because nothing *had* a place. Sure, I'd hear all the drunks and whores out in the alley doing their thing, but it wasn't any worse than listening to the neighbors screaming at each other through the cardboard walls of our apartment, and besides, now that I was an official citizen of the street, we were all more or less like one big happy family anyway.

Only problem was that as summer turned into fall and those big wet storms started blowing in across Long Beach from way out in the Pacific, I was quick to find out that my trusty Cutlass leaked like a rusted-out tin bucket. Who knows how long I might have stayed holed up in that car if I hadn't started worrying about growing mold between my toes and behind my ears from those long, cold, and rainy nights.

Like it or not, I wasn't going to be able to call those four wheels my home much longer. Luckily, I'd been doing a steady business in rock since I'd left home, and I had a big enough bankroll to actually be able to afford a place with four walls and a ceiling. Along with G and a couple of other homies as roommates, I moved into a pad a little further down on Sixty-first, near Linden Avenue, called the Stallion Inn Hotel. It was like a slightly more fly version of a Holiday Inn and had been built a couple of months before we came along, in one of those regular efforts by the city fathers to upgrade the profile of the ghetto.

The Stallion Inn was sure enough an upgrade from the backseat of that Cutlass, and at forty dollars a night split four ways, I could chill there for as long as need be. In fact, it wasn't too long after me and G and the other homies took up residence that a bunch of other niggers in the Rolling Twenties got onto the idea. There were times when gangbangers would take over one entire floor of the Stallion, dealing and partying and generally acting like the place was their own personal penthouse hideaway.

I look back on those times as some of the best of my life, with no responsibilities, nobody to answer to, and nothing more important to do than make my daily quota and spend my profits any way I fucking pleased. It was like the outlaw legend had really come true for me, like the gangsta lifestyle was more than just some Hollywood fantasy to make you forget your own sorry spot in life.

If you wanted to live free, outside the law, and beyond the reach of society, then you could do it. All it took was the balls to pull it off. We did some wicked partying at the Stallion, you can believe that, and the bitches all seemed to know where to go on a Saturday night when they were looking for a little action, a little rock, and maybe a little bumping to set them up right. Snoop's place down at the Stallion—that was the hot spot for a minute there, and I wouldn't have minded if that particular minute would have lasted a lifetime. I was exactly where I wanted to be.

I don't know what the management of that place thought was going on all night long upstairs, over their heads and under their noses, and I'm not so sure they would have cared even if they had figured it out. On the day it opened, the Stallion was bright, shiny, and new, a symbol of hope in a neighborhood that had stopped believing in itself. Six months later, it was just another sorry, run-down, tagged and torn-up flophouse. It just proves what I've already said—things are going to find their own level, no matter how high up or how low down they might start out. A building is the same as a person—you put either one in the middle of a motherfucking ghetto, and chances are they're not going to be bringing up the real-estate value. Sooner or later it's all going to sink down to the same low point. That's just nature's way. Unless, that is, something comes along and burns the whole thing down to the ground. Maybe then there's a chance to start something new, something better.

Like I was saying, the Stallion Inn Hotel got to be Ghetto Central before too long, and with it came a whole lot of competition in the crack trade. Business started shifting from my spot at Sixty-first and Atlantic down closer to the Stallion, and pretty soon you could buy your high right there in the hallways or down at the counter of the coffee shop. I still had my regulars, and I made sure I kept them by giving discounts and markdowns whenever I could—but the other dealers swarming through the 'hood were starting to cut into my profit margins and I knew I had to expand my territory or go out of business.

So I set up a new operation, this time closer to the old 'hood, with some of my schoolyard homies as customers. It wasn't something I was proud of, but the truth is the truth, good, bad, or indifferent, and the truth was I was looking for youngbloods to turn out as crackheads and keep my enterprise alive. Of course, back home, I had the same problem I'd faced at the Six One—moving in on someone else's territory. I managed to solve that problem by hanging out in front of my mama's place until she left for work, then sneaking up the stairs and getting my little brother to let me in. I'd sell dubs off her kitchen table all afternoon long and be gone before she came back. Like I said, it's not something I'm proud of, it's just the way it was.

If you're around the justice system long enough, you're bound to hear the expression "hardened criminal" more than once. And, if you ask me, that's exactly what was happening to Snoop Dogg during those times. The simple truth was, I didn't give a fuck for anybody or anything except myself. If my mama had known what I was doing behind her back, there's no doubt she would have been mad as hell. But her being mad wasn't what mattered. What mattered was her being sad, her realizing she'd lost touch with the son she'd given birth to and done her best to raise up right. It was about letting her down and playing her love like it was worthless. She might have never known what I was doing behind her back—but I knew. And I did it anyway. That's a hard-ass way to be, and I thank God that He·took me out of that condition, gave me self-respect and reminded me that I was His child, with a destiny to follow and a mission to fulfill.

Thinking back on it now, I understand that God was reaching out to me, even then. It wasn't like I saw His face in a cloud or heard His voice thundering in my ear, like fucking Charlton Heston in a Bible movie or something. In my experience, God doesn't work that way. He lets His will and His plan be known to His children by the people and situations He brings across their paths. At the right time, and the right place, there was always someone there to guide me, to point me in the right direction. And even when I chose to go my own way, I still had the clear choice laid out in front of me. It takes time to learn to do the right thing, but God is patient and He'll bring you along, if you let Him.

One of the most important messengers of God, a guardian angel who made a big-time difference in my life from the moment I met her, was my auntie Mary. She really wasn't my aunt; in fact, she wasn't related to me at all, but since I felt a kinship close as family to her, she will always be Auntie Mary in my heart and in my mind.

I'm not sure where Mary came from originally. There were times when I was sure she dropped down from heaven, but by the life she led and the shit she'd been through, she might just as easily have escaped from hell. At the time I knew her, she shared a room in the Stallion with her retarded daughter, who she treated with more love and care and pure affection than most mothers would handle their smartest, most beautiful and talented child. At one time, Mary had another daughter, but I never was exactly sure what had happened to cut short her life. Rumor had it that she had been killed in a shootout at a dope spot, and given that that kind of shit was happening more and more often in those days, it wouldn't surprise me if that were the case. But I never asked Mary about it, first because I didn't want to cause any more pain to a woman who had more than her fair share already, and second because it was none of my business to begin with.

Mary was a good woman. The best. There's no doubt about that. But that didn't mean she took any shit from anyone, no matter what the situation. Before I ever met her, I'd heard a story about how she'd thrown a bottle of acid right in the face of a cheating boyfriend, and when she got herself going on something she didn't like, she could swear so loud and strong she could make the meanest gangbanger in the 'hood blush with embarrassment. She kept a room upstairs from mine at the hotel, and I could hear her on occasion, laying into someone with cuss words I didn't even know they'd invented yet. She'd get this crazy-wild look in her eye when she got mad, and in my mind, that was the Indian side of her, because she'd been born half black and half Apache or some such shit. It was for that reason—and maybe that acid story, too—that I made sure to steer wide of her anytime I saw her boney ass coming down the corridor in front of me.

Except this one time, when she suddenly stepped out from around a corner and boxed me in, holding a finger up so close to my face, I thought she was going to stick it up my nose.

"You the one they call Snoop?" she asked, with a look in her eye that said I better not be lying to her.

"Yes, ma'am," I answered, and it suddenly felt like I was about four years old again and had gotten caught stealing candy from the corner store.

"I hear your mama is fixin' to move," Mary continued. "Is that true?"

Now, the fact is my mama *was* about to move from her apartment because she'd gotten an eviction notice out of the blue, and, while I didn't ask too many questions, I had this sinking feeling it was because I'd been bringing too much crack traffic around there. But how this crazy bitch knew anything about all that—how she even knew who my mama might be—that was a mystery to me.

I was trying to work up the nerve to tell her to mind her own business when Mary gave me another one of those looks, like she'd just caught a cockroach crawling across her clean kitchen floor. "You fixin' to help your mama move?" she asked.

To be honest, I hadn't thought about it. My mama and I hadn't been getting along so well since I moved out of the house, and I sure didn't consider it my duty to be working up a sweat hauling her heavy furniture down all those flights of stairs. I opened my mouth and was just about to tell this half-breed, acid-throwing mental case to mind her own damn business when Mary brought that crooked finger of hers even closer to my face, this time like she was going to reach down my throat and start feeling around to see if I had a heart.

"She's your mama," Mary hissed, like steam coming out of an overheated radiator. "You mean to tell me that you ain't gonna help your mama when she be needing you the most? *Shame* on you, nigger! That ain't no way for a motherfuckin' son to be treatin' his motherfuckin' mama!"

I swallowed hard, all my gangbanger attitude shrinking down to about the size of a kernel of unpopped corn. I wasn't a crack dealer anymore. I wasn't a Crip or a Rolling Twenty or a big, bad gangsta. I was just a little piss-ass kid who ought to be ashamed of himself for treating his mama that way.

"I was . . ." I stammered, "just on my way over there now."

"See that you hurry," Mary said, backing up to give me just enough room to escape. "And don't be hanging out with none of your asshole friends on the way over, neither. Your mama needs you, boy!"

Mary was right, of course, and it felt good to just suddenly show up on the doorstep and see the look of happiness on my mama's face when she saw me again. My mama sure enough did need me that day. But she wasn't the only one lacking for something. I needed a mama, too—someone to look out for me and point me in the right direction and show me the difference between what's the right thing to do and what's the bullshit thing to do. And since I wouldn't let my real mama do her job, God had given me another one named Auntie Mary.

Cold hoopin' it at a
charity game.

chapter twelve

hen I think back now on those times, I realize that God gave me all kinds of protection and provision that I didn't even have a clue about. I don't know what would have happened to me if there weren't people like Auntie Mary and my man Warren G in my life. I'd probably be in jail . . . or worse. The truth is, I'd rather not think about it. It's better all around just to give thanks to my Creator for sending me guides and guards and watchmen to look out after me and point me in the right direction so I could accomplish what I was set on this earth to do.

That doesn't make me special or unique. I know for sure that if you looked around your own life you'd see those same kinds of God-given homeboys and family connections that are there to bring you along and help you fulfill your destiny. I'm even sure that you got enemies in your life, those thorns in your side, that God is also using to make you a better person. Because life is never just about what you got going *for* you, but what you got going *against* you, too. It's the things you've got to overcome that make you a better person, and if you haven't found that out yet, you will soon enough. Word.

But of all the people that God has put in my path for good, there is one that means more to me than all the rest put together. Check it out—everybody needs a mama and daddy; everyone needs a homeboy they can count on like G and a crew to call their own, like I had with the Rolling Twenties. But you have all that, and all the scrilla you can handle besides, and you still won't have shit unless you've got someone special to share it all with.

And that's what I got with Shanté, my wife, my soulmate, the mother of my children, and a true-blue homegirl through thick and thin.

I have to admit to feeling a little hesitation when it comes to talking about Shanté to a bunch of strangers, even if it is just words on a page. Most parts of the Snoop Dogg saga I don't mind letting loose with—you take the good with the bad and that's what makes up a whole life story. Mine included. But when it comes to turning that bright spotlight on someone else, especially someone who's got every right to live her life free from the kind of celebrity bullshit I've got to put up with on a daily basis . . . well, that's a different situation all together.

As far as I'm concerned, my wife is entitled to as much privacy as any other regular citizen who's just about raising their family and enjoying the simple pleasures that life has to offer. She didn't ask to be married to a rap star and she didn't ask to have her past, present, and future put under a microscope for everyone to dissect, like a frog in biology class. That's just the way things turned out, and I consider part of my responsibility to her and to my children to keep that shit as far away from their front door as I can.

But, on the other hand, this is the story of my life, and Shanté is a big part of that story, like it or not. So, baby, I hope you'll forgive me for having to include you in all this. People want to know, and what people want to know, people are going to find out, one way or the other. It's better that they hear it from me than that they start making shit up on their own.

But now that I got that out of the way, let me be straight up with you all—Shanté has got her own game together. Always has and always will. When I try to describe her, all I come up with are words that don't seem to go together but somehow add up to her personality. Shanté is sweet and innocent, but she knows what's what. She's kind and generous, but she won't stand for being taken advantage of. She's patient, but she doesn't put up with shit; she's understanding but never gets played; independent but loyal; a lover *and* a fighter; the best friend you could ask for and the worst enemy you could make. My wife is one in a million, but she always makes me feel like the special one. Here's to you, Shanté. I love you, baby.

I wish I could tell you it was one of those love-at-first-sight scenes you're always seeing in the movies when Shanté and I first laid eyes on each other. The media makes a business of feeding us all those romantic fantasies and it gets to where we don't think it's the real thing unless it happens like they show it to us, running through a field of daisies in slow motion.

I'm here to tell you there aren't any motherfucking daisy fields in my neck of the 'hood. We've got sidewalks and vacant lots and sometimes, if you're lucky, you can find yourself a corner of King Park that isn't overrun with homeboys or whores working their game. Maybe love in the ghetto is different from the way it's played anywhere else, though if you ask me, even if you *could* find yourself a daisy field, that's not going to guarantee true romance any more than a movie can promise you a happily-ever-after life. Reality has a way of turning all that make-believe bullshit inside out, and sooner or later you'll be waking up to the cold, hard facts that love at first sight doesn't last forever and what it takes to get through with someone is hanging in, one day at a time, for better or worse, till death do you part.

If anything, I believe it might be even harder to find love and hang on to it when you're living on the edge of survival, like so many niggers are doing all across this country. If poverty and crime and violence teaches you one thing, it's to take your pleasure where you can find it. Most of us don't have the leisure time for all that flirting and teasing and hide-and-seek that's supposed to go with romance. Word up: in the ghetto, love means getting into some bitch's panties, and if that means she ends up with a baby that's got your face, well, that's on her. Nobody's around to teach us that love means commitment and sex means responsibility and having babies means supporting a family. We're all out there looking for someone to care for, and to care for us, and we think that when some young bitch spreads her legs that means something special. But the truth is, it doesn't mean shit. It just means we don't know where to find what it is we're looking for. We're sure enough babies having babies and that's a tragedy no matter how you look at it.

I guess what I'm getting at is that the odds are against most homies finding out what real love is all about. But like I said, God is looking out after me. And that's why He sent me Shanté, even if it took me a long while to figure that out.

Shanté Taylor is a child of Long Beach, just like me, only from another 'hood across town that was a little better off than where I was banging. Her street had little houses with little yards and maybe a lemon or an orange tree out in the back. And, if you didn't look too closely at the iron bars on the windows or the triple-locked doors, you might think that where she grew up was just a normal middle-class hang that somehow got passed over with all the drive-bys and crackheads and gangstas from across town. But it wasn't true. Shanté's life had that same shadow over it that all the rest of us in the ghetto had. That just came with the territory of being black and living in America. Nothing was going to change that, no matter what kind of fruit trees you had growing in your yard.

She was a couple of years behind me coming up in school, which meant that I didn't get much of a chance to notice her in class or out on the playground. You know how it is, when you're a youngblood, all you're thinking about is getting older and taller, or getting to the next grade or when you are going to get to run with the big boys. Anyone younger or smaller than you might just as well not exist, especially some nappy-headed, knock-kneed little girl from outside the 'hood.

I guess you could say what happened to Shanté and me was the opposite of love at first sight. It was more like love at second and tenth and nineteenth sight. Every step was so slow and gradual, I don't believe either one of us knew for sure what was happening, and speaking for myself, I couldn't exactly tell you when was the first time I really *noticed* her in a way that would stick with me. Don't get me wrong—there's a hundred different scenes in my memory that have her somewhere in the background. I can remember more than once seeing her big wide smile on the sidelines of a Pop Warner football game, or catching her eye in the hallway as we headed for our lockers between classes. I can clearly picture her standing around on the street outside Lafayette Elementary with a bunch of her homegirls, laughing and carrying on and posing with a hand on her hip like sassy young ladies do when they start to notice that the homeboys are interested. I can see her down at Norm's after a game or a movie on a Saturday night, sipping Coke through a long straw and sharing a basket of fries with some of her crew. And I can watch her, even now, sitting at the window of a school bus as it pulled away to take her back to her side of town.

Like I said, I've got a head full of memories of Shanté. I just couldn't tell you which one came first and in what order the others followed. In one way, it was like Shanté was *always* somewhere in my life, up close or off a little distance, and as time went on, she got to be more and more in the middle of things. One minute, she was just some little punk kid running wild on the playground, shouting and laughing, just like I had done back in the day. The next minute she was a face in the crowd that stood out from the others—with her dark eyes and her clear skin and that same wide smile that, after a while, seemed to follow me wherever I went.

Then, the next thing you know, I was starting to look for her when I'd notice that she wasn't around, and got to wondering where she was when I couldn't pick her on the playground. Nobody ever said to me, "There she is. That's the one. She's going to be your wife one day." It wasn't like that and I wouldn't have believed it even if it had been. It was all just a natural progression that got me, somewhere along the way, to realizing what it seemed like I'd known all along.

A big step on the way there was when I got to be counting on Shanté as a friend. We'd gotten to talking during lunch and after school, and once in a while I'd ask her to go out to the movies with me or come watch me play hoops at King Park. It was no big deal . . . at least not for me. It wasn't like I was asking her out on a *date* or anything. It was more just like, well, the right move to make. I liked being around her. It felt relaxed and there was nothing I had to prove to her. She seemed interested in what I had to say and when she listened to all my bullshit, I got the feeling she was *really* listening, and not just waiting for her turn to talk. The fact is, Shanté isn't much of a talker to begin with. She's quiet and keeps her thoughts and feelings to herself—that is, until she's sure she can trust you with what she's got to say, and even then, she won't tell you unless you ask.

The one feeling I remember best from being around her was that here was one homegirl who was really and truly *for* me—on my side and in my corner. It was like she wanted the best for me and was keeping her fingers crossed that I'd get where I needed to go, even if I wasn't sure, from one day to the next, where exactly that might be. Before I ever knew I loved her, or ever thought about asking her to be my wife, Shanté was my friend, my number one homegirl, and the one person I trusted with my deepest and darkest secrets.

Now, depending on how you feel about women, you might be suspecting that Shanté had it all planned out that way from the beginning. Like, first she got me to notice her; then she got me to like her; then she got me to trust her; and after that, it was as easy to reel me in as a fish on a hook. A lot of brothers will tell you that bitches run the world, anyway, pulling all the strings from behind the scenes and leading men around by their dicks. Maybe that's so and maybe it's not. But as far as Shanté working her game on me, that's something you'd have to ask her . . . except that if I ever see you snooping around my house asking my wife personal questions, I'll be sure to sic the dogs on your ass.

Let's just leave it like this: Shanté and I found each other. That was God's will. It didn't happen overnight and it didn't happen in a fucking field of daisies. What we got is real and we work it out every day, in the here and now, with no magic kingdoms and happily ever afters. It's about believing in each other, building something together, and being on each other's side. I don't know any other way to do it. Do you?

Of course, that doesn't mean Shanté and I haven't made more than our share of mistakes. We've been together too long not to have fumbled the ball, lost some yardage, and had a penalty flag dropped on us. To start with, I'd be a lying motherfucker if I claimed I've been faithful to my woman from the first day I finally realized she *was* my woman. The plain truth is, even during this time in my life, running with the Twenties and dealing dub off my spot, there was more than a few times I'd take advantage of some poor crackwhore who wanted to trade pussy for rock. I've already copped to that, and not just in the pages of this book. Shanté knows about my past; she knows the kind of shit I'm capable of and she knows that, just like everyone else on this planet, Snoop Dogg has got a struggle between good and evil going on inside of him.

But it wasn't just in my old gangbanging days that I did some unauthorized bumping. Any rap star who tells you he hasn't picked a fine young thing out of the crowd at a concert and told his roadie to bring her backstage after the show . . . well, let's just say that motherfucker is playing you for a chump. Of course, a situation can get a little out of control on the road, and sometimes, if it doesn't, you might nudge it along a little bit in that direction all by yourself. You can take it from Snoop, because I don't lie: there are some fine women out there who like nothing better than to fuck a big-time rap star, then go back to their homegirls and brag about it. That's the name of the game and everyone plays it. I don't care who you are . . . or who you pretend to be.

The difference between me and those other assholes is that I'm not pretending to be someone I'm not. I'm Snoop Dogg, goddamnit, and my motherfucking reputation precedes me wherever I go. I don't answer to anyone, and that includes Shanté, my loving wife and the mother of my fine children. What I choose to do I take full responsibility for, before my family and almighty God, and when I choose not to do it, it's because sometimes there's more important things in life than getting your dick wet every time some bitch shakes her ass in your direction.

I tell Shanté the same thing I tell you. She knows what's up, and how she deals with it is between her and me. But since we're on the subject, I got a suggestion for you, if you should ever find yourself in the particular situation I'm talking about. You ask yourself who it is that stood by you through the best and the worst; ask yourself who's the one person you can trust when all your homies have turned their backs on you; ask yourself what it means to betray a friendship and violate a trust. If you can answer all those questions honestly and that bitch with the tight skirt in the front row *still* looks too good to pass by, then it's on you. She may look nice, but you'll pay the price. Take it from Snoop Dogg. Then do what you've got to do.

chapter thirteen

Gangsta lean.

chapter thirteen

Big changes come from little changes. Things you might not think are important at the time can turn out to be what it takes to push you off in a whole other direction. Someone might say something to you, something casual and off the cuff, and it turns out to be the right word at the right time to make the right move. Or some insignificant event might happen that you hardly notice, never mind pay any heed to. But then other circumstances start to happen behind that first one and you get that snowball effect with things piling up on top of each other and you look back and realize that, hey, that one little moment was the start of it all.

When I look back now, I see one of those very same moments coming along in my life, one that would make all the difference to everything else that came along after. It was no big deal at the time, nothing to call attention to itself and let me know my life was about to take a one-eighty. It was nothing more than a seed, really, planted in a corner of my life and waiting until that time when all the conditions were right and the roots and branches could start growing.

The year was 1988, the time was late summer, during those lazy days in Cali when you start to feel the seasons change and a soft breeze comes in off the ocean and blows all that stale, smoggy air back up against the mountains. Life in the 'hood was slowing down, and the homeboys were sitting back for a minute, taking a deep breath between the party days of summer and the cooler, quieter days of winter up ahead. Youngbloods were getting ready to go back to school, the traffic at Six One was slow and steady, and even the twenty-four-hour action at the Stallion seemed to be easing up.

I guess the best way to sum up that time in my life is to remind myself of the music that was coming out of car radios on the street and boom boxes on the beach. Music always brings back a time and place better than just about anything else, and we've all got our own Top 10 list of golden oldies to remind us of better days.

For me, the bomb album of that whole year was *The Great Adventures of Slick Rick.* Up to then, rap music had mostly been about niggers bragging on themselves and bagging on each other, but Rick had something different going, and to me it was a real inspiration. On *The Great Adventures,* Rick created real characters, different voices with different points of view that told stories about life in the ghetto that were funny and nasty and true. I liked what Rick was putting down because it showed me that rap could really represent a whole range of emotions and attitudes and characters that most musical styles couldn't touch. Shit, Rick was a character all by himself, with that eye patch and those jumbo-sized gold rings and that funky English accent that gave everything he said a special twist unique to him. Word up: Slick Rick was the bomb.

It was listening to his raps that got me back into thinking about my own musical inclinations and, from there, trying to make something happen with the talent God had given me. It wasn't even so much that I dared to dream I could one day make a career from rhymes and rhythms—it was just that what I heard Rick doing I wanted to do myself, only putting my own spin on it. I know I'm not the only dude who ever heard a rap record and thought to himself, *I can do that!* But there's a difference between thinking and doing, and it comes down to one thing: confidence.

And the reality was, I didn't have a whole lot of that particular commodity at the time. Homies like G and Nate Dogg were always telling me I had skills, but they were my friends—what else were they going to say? Besides, if they had ears that were good enough to pick out a real rapper, what the hell were they doing scraping by on the street with me? Half of me wanted to believe that I had what it took to make a run at the rap game, but it was the other half that just kept telling me, *Who you tryin' to fool, nigger?* And that was the voice I believed.

Anyway, by the fall of '88, I didn't have much reason to look forward to any big changes happening for Snoop Dogg. It was like my life had fallen into a groove that ran so deep it would have taken an eight-pointer on the Richter scale to knock me out of that track. I was a drug dealer, a gangbanger, a citizen of the street with all the privileges and problems that go along with the territory. One thing was for damn sure: I wasn't about to kick over my gig to go chasing some slim chance of rap stardom. That was for suckers and fools, and I was neither one of those.

Or so I thought. Sometimes it's the things you can't see on the road ahead of you that get you in trouble and not the big bumps you've got the sense enough to steer around. In my mind, I had it all figured out. I was a Rolling Twenty. I belonged to the crew and the crew belonged to me. I had what you might call job security, and there was just no reason to believe that things would ever be any different. People weren't going to stop getting high, were they? And someone had to provide the means for them to get there, didn't they? Like I said, it was all about supply and demand, and I was a ghetto entrepreneur doing his part for the American economy.

Or some such bullshit. The truth is, I told myself all kinds of lies to justify what I was doing, and as long as no one called me on it, I could just keep hiding from the truth. The truth was, I was living on borrowed time. Sooner or later, something was going to give, and when it did, you can be sure I was the one who'd be doing the giving . . . until it hurt.

But while I could lie to myself, God had put people in my life who would see though all the trash I was talking and who wanted something better for me than I wanted for myself. They wanted me to go for my dream, even when I didn't know what that dream might be; to sharpen my talent, even when I wasn't sure I had any talent to begin with; and to look for something higher in my life, even if I couldn't tell which way was up.

Most of those people you already know—G and Auntie Mary and Shanté, along with some other homeboys and girls who know who they are. Any one of them would have stepped up for me in a heartbeat and done whatever it took to make me see that I had more to live for, more to strive for, than I ever gave myself credit for. But for me to be able to hear what they were saying, I had to be listening, and that was something I hadn't learned how to do yet. So everyone that meant anything to me just pulled back and bided their time, waiting for the right moment.

That moment came in early September of '88. By that time Shanté and I had been going together, more or less officially, a good while and I wanted to formally introduce her to all my homies and the Six One crew, let them all know that this was my special lady and that from then on, she came under my jurisdiction, so to speak. So I put out the word that I was throwing a party up on the top floor of the Stallion, where most of the rooms were already taken up by the Twenties and where we could be sure we weren't going to be disturbed when we got it going on.

Actually, looking back on it all, I'm not so sure I was as interested in showing Shanté around as I was in just having a big old party, but any excuse would do the trick and I knew she'd feel good if we rolled out something big in her honor. So I slipped Auntie Mary some bills to cook up a mess of food, laid in some gin and juice, and put out the word that there was a party about to be going down.

The only thing left to take care of was the entertainment. I could have just spun discs all night long, but I was really in the mood for something special, and what could be more special than live music hired just for the occasion? I started asking around to a get a lead on some group that might be available, and the first homey I asked was G. After all, he was tight with Dr. Dre, and if anyone knew what was up with the bomb sounds in L.A., it was going to be that nigger.

But G put another idea in my head. Remember how I was saying that in school he and I and Nate Dogg had gotten together just messing around? Well, nothing much had come from trying it out that time around, and I'd kind of chalked it up to the foolishness that young-bloods get themselves into when they don't know any better than to try out something just for the hell of it.

But G didn't see it that way. In fact, ever since that time he'd been trying to get himself gigs as a DJ and had been making the rounds all over Long Beach, East L.A., and Compton. He knew what was out there, who the competition was, and where it was at for young rappers who were looking for a break. And it was in his mind that the time had come for us to catch a break.

G's plan was simple—me and Nate would rap, he'd be the DJ, and we'd be our own damn entertainment at the party. Only, I wasn't buying it . . . at least not at first. I was more interested in getting somebody with a little experience under their belt so at least the people would be entertained. I had no interest in dodging beer bottles if what we could come up with didn't measure up to the party spirit that night.

But G stayed on it and rode me hard about the idea. Remember I told you he was a nagger? I promised to think on it, but I was pretty sure I wasn't down for the game—that is, until I talked to Auntie Mary about it. There's been lots of times since, thinking back on the way that whole party came to be, that I wondered whether G and Mary hadn't cooked up something between themselves, just to get me to go along. I don't know that Mary had ever heard me rap before or not, but it didn't much matter. She made it clear enough that if I didn't give it try I'd have to be answering to her, personally, and she was in no mood to listen to my lame-ass excuses. If she was going to cook, I was going to rap . . . and that was that.

I knew enough to see that I'd come up against a force I couldn't reckon with. To get her off my back, I told her I'd try out a few things with G and Nate, just to see how it went. Now, it had been a good long while since me and my brothers had done anything together more creative than smoking chronic, and the afternoon we first got together, in a toolshed back of Nate's place, we were more than a little rusty.

But even in those first couple of hours, I think we all realized that something different was going on. Whatever it was we had been trying to do back in the day was mostly based on what we were hearing on the radio—East Coast rap that had a certain hard edge and attitude that, while it might have been cool, was hard for us to relate to directly. What had gone down since that time was a whole lot of hometown rappers coming up through the ranks—most especially N.W.A—and while maybe their sound was a little more Compton than L.B., it still had that definite West Coast feel.

But there was more going on between the three of us than just picking up on the L.A. vibe. If I had to describe it—and I guess I do—I'd have to say it was a combination of a couple of different things. Up front, there was Slick Rick, a nigger who had done a lot for me just in terms of sparking ideas and opening up the possibilities of what rap could say and how it could say it. Rick was slick all right, and he blazed a trail that a lot of us would follow.

The second big influence at that time was in the music I'd grown up listening to. The soul and R&B that my mama had been playing ever since I was in the cradle had made its mark on my own style, no question about it. If singers like Al Green were anything, they were mellow, taking a song nice and easy, without rushing through the words or trying to get across the message by sheer lung power. For those cats, a whisper was always better than a scream. So since I wasn't interested in trying to cop my licks from the N.W.A bag of tricks, I just naturally turned back to the first sounds I could remember. And those sounds were all about taking your time and taking it easy.

The last thing that I think made a big difference to the raps we were laying down had to do with what we were smoking. When Nate, G, and I first tried working together, we may have been familiar with weed, but you wouldn't exactly call it being on a first-name basis. This time around, we had a couple years of smoking experience under us, so we'd built what you might call a foundation of mellowness, an unhurried, unhassled mood that you can only get when you've been a steady smoker for a while.

So, as best I can describe it, all these things just came together at the same time and place out in that toolshed. The first thing we noticed was that our natural inclination was to slow things down and not to try and run as many words as we could together just to show that we could flow off the tip of our tongue. We wanted to make every rhyme count, and that meant the rhythm had to be something you could groove to without getting your pulse pounding.

The next thing that came clear was that the raps we were coming up with were about the things we knew, the world we lived in, and the everyday joys and sorrows that we all had in common. There wasn't all that much that was politically militant or socially relevant about our first flows. We might have agreed with niggers who were singing "Fuck the police," but we felt more comfortable when we were singing "Party all night long." It's not that one is legit and the other isn't. That's just where we were coming from at the time and all we knew to rap about was what was going on in *our* lives. We wanted to have a good time and it seemed like the best way to do that was to make up rhymes about having a good time. Doesn't take a motherfucking genius to figure that one out.

I can't say for sure, but looking back, my guess is that the reason that music sounded so good to us was because it came from someplace real inside. We weren't trying to be someone we weren't, or trying to prove something we couldn't. We're were just hoping that, going in, we wouldn't make goddamn fools of ourselves, and the only way we knew how to do that was to say exactly what we felt, what was on our minds, and make it all sound real. The truth is, I don't know that we thought much about it at all, at least in any deliberate way. When that first session was over, the three of us were more surprised by what had come out than anyone else might have been. But I will tell you this: we knew a good thing when we heard it.

It was that excitement that kept us going over the next couple of days, working hard to come up with enough material to put together a legit act for the party. I found myself writing most of the raps, and while I couldn't tell you now the name of a single one, I knew I was tapping into a part of my soul that had never been touched before. On more than one night, I'd stay up until dawn, with the rowdy rooms of the Stallion quiet and sleeping around me, writing down my rhymes so fast I'd get cramps in my fingers. For the first time ever, I actually started to believe that maybe what G had been telling me was right all along. Maybe I *did* have a talent—a talent that could take me further than I'd ever dreamed I could go.

But believing is different from doing, and when the time finally came for us to step out in front of our homeboys and girls and do our thing, about all I could hear was my heart pounding, so loud I thought it was the bass drum on the track G had laid down. That first show is nothing but a blur to me now. The only thing I remember, and I remember it so clear it could have happened yesterday, was when we finished, and the roar of blood pumping through my ears settled down enough so I could hear what was going on around me. It was the sound of clapping and shouting and whistling and people calling out my name as loud as they could. I'd never heard a noise like that before, but I knew right then that I wanted to hear it again, as much as I could, for as long as I could.

I looked around at Nate and G and they were grinning so wide I thought their faces might crack. But the face I remember best was the one over in the back of the room, bright and shining and full of encouragement. Shanté was proud of me, proud to be my woman. And right about then, I was so happy, I didn't even think twice about whether I deserved it.

Me, my pops, and some
of my signifying
homeskillets.

chapter fourteen

I kept getting feedback from that party for the next couple of days, niggers I didn't even know coming up to me on the street and acting like I was something special all of a sudden, hitting me up for tapes and wanting the 411 on when I was going to be rapping again.

All that attention felt good, but to tell you the truth, if no one had ever said another word to me about my big debut, it wouldn't have made the slightest bit of difference. I was sold on myself, and maybe for the first time in my life knew exactly where I was going and what I was going for. Rapping did something for me that nothing else ever had— not Pop Warner football, not being in the Six One crew, not making big bank selling dub rocks. It was like I'd had an itch way down deep on the inside someplace that I'd never been able to scratch and I'd had it so long I didn't even know it *needed* to be scratched. But the minute I opened my mouth and the freestyle started to flow, strong and true and straight from my heart through my grille, I understood that I'd been missing something my whole life, something I couldn't put a name to until I'd found it. Rap was suddenly the meaning of my life— and the middle of my world.

You might be wondering why this knowledge didn't drop for me sooner, back in school when Nate and G and I first started playing around with music. I don't have an answer for that, except to say that there's a time and place for everything and until that September night in '88, my time and place hadn't come together. Maybe back in the day I was too young to appreciate how rap gave me a way to express what the deepest part of myself was all about; maybe I was too caught up in sports and bumping and video games to even pay much attention. Or maybe it was just that I never really thought I could make it in the big, bad world of professional music, that I was missing the self-confidence it took to make others believe in you.

If I had to guess, I'd put that last one down as the main reason. Rap stars like Slick Rick were in a class by themselves, a world apart from the regular run of cousins scraping by on the street. And even though you could tell by their raps that those hit-making niggers knew what was what in our world, there was just no way we could reach up and be a part of what *they* were all about: limos and fine bitches and big bodyguards clearing a path to get you inside the five-star restaurant where the white waiters bowed and scraped and brought out the vintage champagne with a white towel over their arm for their very special guest. Where I came from that just didn't happen—not to me and not to anyone I'd ever known.

But after that night, something changed inside of me. I actually began to believe that if I worked hard and kept focused and caught a few breaks, maybe it could *happen* for me. Maybe I could get to where those other homies had gotten. If it could happen for them, why couldn't it happen for me?

Of course, there's about a million different reasons why the odds are stacked against you from jump . . . about one reason for every fucking rap wannabe that's out there trying to get *his* shit across. Word: anything that's got that big of a payoff at the back end is sure to have a whole mob of motherfuckers crowding up front at the starting gate. To say that the competition is fierce in the rap game isn't exactly the Cronkite. The way the game is played you've got to have determination, patience, and a take-no-prisoners attitude to even get yourself noticed by the guardians of the gate. And even then, if you don't have a whole lot of luck going for you, you might as well just walk away now and get yourself a straight gig selling shoes or delivering pizza. Because no matter how much you plan or scheme or try to boost the odds up in your favor, success in rap music is just like I said before—it's about being in the right place at the right time with the right sound.

Naturally, I didn't know any of that going in. And I don't think it would have made a whole lot of difference even if I had. The truth is this: I wasn't interested in rap as a way to get driven around downtown in the back of limo with a dukey rope and briefcase full of broccoli and some fly bitch on her knees tending to my jammy. That all sounded fine, if that's what got you going, but what got Snoop Dogg going was the pure thrill of finding the rhymes in time and sound that got around. Check it out—rap is my way of expressing who I am, where I come from, and where I'm going. It's my soul that speaks when I step up to the mic, and the words and rhythms are my way of telling the world that I'm here, that I matter, and that I deserve respect. That's what I got in touch with that night at the party, and I've never lost the connection since. So if I made ten dollars or ten million dollars from my music, it wouldn't much matter. I'd still be doing it. And not just because I want to, but because I've *got* to.

Nothing was going to stop me from chasing after my dream with everything I had, and in the days and weeks after the party, I felt like I'd been handed the answer to a riddle I been trying to crack from the cradle:

Q: *Why did God make Snoop Dogg?*

A: *God made Snoop Dogg to rap.*

And once I knew that for sure, it was just a matter of moving in the right direction as fast as I could, going from point A to point B in a direct line, with no delays and no distractions. I was on my way.

The only problem was, there were a couple of unscheduled stops along the route . . .

The hyped-up energy I was running on since the party was enough to get G and Nate Dogg revved and ready to go along for the ride. The three of us started laying down big plans, taking about demos and deals like we already knew what the fuck it was all about.

The fact is, we didn't know shit. G had given up passing tapes along to his half brother Dre right about the time I'd lost interest in making them, back when I was still in school. I don't know whether Dre ever heard a single note we did off those first couple of tries. I sure hope not.

I don't remember much about the raps we came up with back in the day, but what I *do* remember makes me hope they've been burned or buried a long time ago. Like I said, I just wasn't ready to make my move back then, and you could tell by the quality of the shit I came up with.

This time around, it was going to be different. The first thing G and Nate and I did was to what you might call put an official authorization on our partnership. We decided we had to have a name. After a lot of bullshit sessions, blowing through a lot of cheeba, we finally came up with *213,* which was the L.A. telephone area code at the time before it broke off into a half dozen different combinations. It was a little bit of wishful thinking if you ask me: I mean, what made us so cocksure we could go out and represent the whole motherfucking city of Los Angeles to the world at large? The Wreckin' Cru' and N.W.A had already blazed that trail, but, like I said, we had nothing if we didn't have a lot of balls . . . so 213 it was. Like they put it down over in the brown part of town, we were after the whole enchilada.

So now we had a name. All we needed next was about ten songs, a record deal, and a nationwide tour to let the world know that the Next Big Thing was finally on the scene. What we settled for, instead, was the same old toolshed out back of Nate's crib, where we spent more sweaty hours than I care to remember getting down the basics of our game.

Like so many other things in life, the best rap is the kind that sounds simple and effortless . . . like it doesn't take any trouble at all for you to stand up and just let the flow happen. But, as anyone from a ballet dancer to a movie star to a stand-up comic will tell you, making it look easy is the hardest thing in the world. It's all about finding your identity, your style, the thing you've got that nobody else does. You can work your ass off to bite the raps of Slick Rick or N.W.A or the Sugarhill Gang or anybody else you might admire, and, sure enough, they say that imitation is the sincerest form of flattery. But the name of the game is to get good enough to where other niggers are imitating *you,* and that means you've got to find something original in yourself to offer. And if it doesn't show itself right away, you've just got to keep working at it until one day you come down to make a basic decision: have I got something new to bring to the table or am I just jerking off myself and everyone around else around me?

Once you make that decision, the rest is easy. You either give up on the dream or work your ass off to develop what you got. There's no shortcuts, no cheats, and no microwavable creativity that you can cop. It's about working hard when the only thing that might be keeping you going is believing that if you *keep* going, you might actually be going somewhere, and get there someday.

And that's what we were doing out there in that toolshed from sunup to sundown, twenty-four seven. I've read in the rap magazines where they describe my style as "a vicious, lazy drawl," and I take that as a compliment. I've got my own approach, it's 100 percent mine, and while it might be often imitated, it's never been duplicated. There's a whole lot of Snoop sound-alikes out there these days, but I guarantee you that from the first time you hear me start to rap on one of my records, you know exactly who you're listening to. It's the Snoop Sound, and if you could put it in a bottle and label it, you'd be as rich as I am. Only don't bother. It's nothing you can manufacture. It's who I am, my essence, and I discovered it during those long hours with my brothers in that little overheated lean-to, with busted mowers and socket sets and claw hammers hanging off the walls.

Slowly, as the weeks went by, we all got closer and closer to that moment of truth, that time I was talking about when you ask yourself if it's worth it and whether you've got enough talent to keep pushing for something that's bigger than the three of you put together. The funny thing is, when we got to that point, we must have breezed right by it, because none of us even brought up the possibility that we were maybe wasting our time. We had something special together. We knew it. All we had to do now was convince the rest of the world.

It was right around then, coming up on the holiday season, when we started playing out for the odd party or Crip Christmas get-together. And every time, we got the same reaction—niggers went crazy. It was more than them just being loyal to homies from the 'hood, although I'm sure that had a lot to do with it, at least at first. But as time went on, people were digging us for what we were, the sound that we put down and the style that we had worked so hard to make our own. We were getting what you'd call a following.

But to be honest, as far as Long Beach went, we were pretty much in

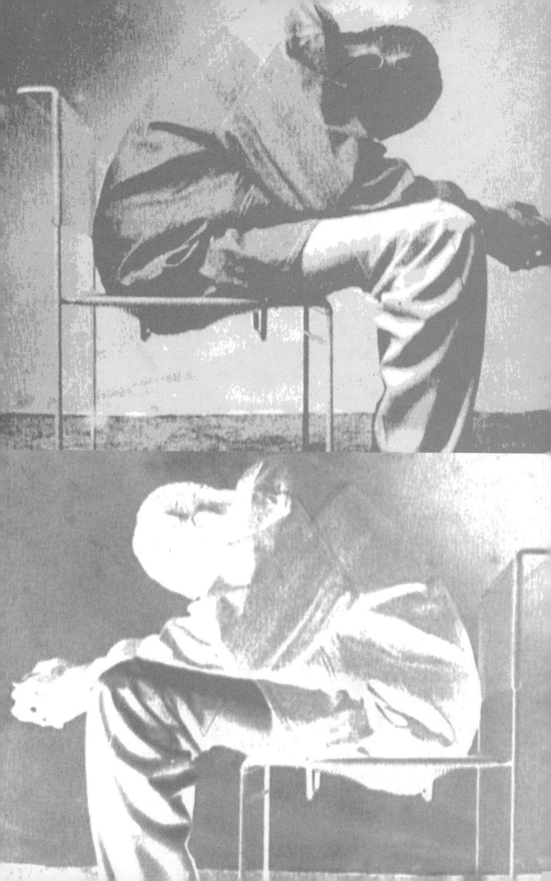

a category all our own. School-age youngbloods maybe got together to try out their chops for kicks, but none of them had put much effort behind it and most of the time the only appeal they had was that they were trying so hard. There just wasn't anyone else as old as we three were, with the same kind of gang credentials, that were as serious about what they were doing as the 213. If there was ever going to be an L.B. style of rap, it was going to be up to us to make it happen.

And that's exactly what we were trying to do. Rap music, even these days, is as much about where you're from as what you're saying. It's about being true to your 'hood, your crew, and the niggers you came up with. A brother from Compton or South Central may be partial to a sound coming out of New York or Atlanta or even right across town from where he hangs. But he sure as hell isn't going to let anyone else know that. You stay loyal to your roots and the rap that gets tapped from those roots. That's the way it is, and that's the way it's always going to be.

Who knows how much longer we could have kept climbing with all the energy we brought to the game? Who know how things might have turned out if they hadn't turned out the way they did? Who knows . . . well, you get the drift. *Nobody* knows what might have been or what's going to be. The best we can do is tell the truth about how it was and let God take care of the rest. 213 was my ticket to the future; at least that's the way I thought about it. But I was about to take another turn on the road to my destiny, one that was going to lead me down along the darkest valleys of my life before I'd be able to climb back out and catch the light of day.

It's something I got used to a long time ago. God's in charge, not Snoop Dogg. You can do it His way or you can not do it at all. Either way, He's got the last word. And that's fine by me.

Since I'd been spending so much time in that shed with G and Nate polishing our licks for 213, my rock business with Six One had dropped way off. I got to where I was owing more money than I was comfortable with for inventory I didn't have the time or—to tell you the truth—the inclination to move. Some of my customers were starting to complain, and it got to where I realized I was going to have to take care of business if I wanted to have a business left to take care of.

I decided that, no matter how much I wanted to practice the new flows me and my homies were putting down, I was going to have to hit the corner and move some of my stash.

It was six o'clock on a Friday night, prime time for maximum sales, with people getting off work, heading home, and hoping to lay in a supply for the weekend. I pulled together a good pile of dubs and hid them in my usual spot up at the Twenties house, then made it down to Sixty-first and took my regular place under the light by the Laundromat, where I could see and be seen.

Right from jump, I had more action than I could handle. It was like my regulars had been holding back, waiting for me to show and ready to make up for lost time. For the first couple of hours, all I did was hustle back and forth between my stash and my corner, turning dubs and making change.

The sun was going down over the building, throwing long shadows across the street. I remember humming along to flow we'd been working on that afternoon as I tried to keep on top of the trade, and thinking about something special I wanted to get for Shanté . . . I had my eye on a fine, foxy leather coat and some sexy lingerie and was trying to decide between the two when a carful of college kids from over at Cal State Dominguez Hills rolled to a stop.

I recognized a couple of those caveboys in the backseat, even though it was getting dark by this time and hard to see the expressions on their faces. I always trusted my instincts when I was out on the corner, and most times, if I couldn't look someone straight in the eye, I'd shine them on. But, like I said, I was distracted that particular evening and wasn't paying a whole lot of attention, even when they placed an order that was a whole lot bigger than usual.

When I got back to my stash I realized I'd be out of dubs after this deal and decided to call it quits for the night. Hell, it was still early. Maybe I could round up G and Nate and we could get in a few hours of practice.

It was that exact thought that I had on my mind when I got back to the corner and, leaning in the open window on the passenger side of the car, passed over a fistful of rock and held out my hand for the money.

Suddenly, from every corner of the street, I saw big men in windbreakers and sunglasses rushing toward me. I straightened up and for a heartbeat and a half looked around me, wondering where the bust was going down. Then, before I could pull another breath, they had drawn down on me and I was staring up the barrels of a dozen police service revolvers and a bunch of other heavy-duty firepower coming up from around the other side of the car. A squad of berries came screaming around the corner and screeched to a stop at the scene of the crime.

"Freeze!" one of the cops shouted, but he didn't need to tell me. I couldn't have moved if I'd wanted to. My feet were stuck to the pavement and all I could feel was that fistful of dub vials getting bigger and bigger in my hand as I stood there with a dumb look on my face and a feeling in my gut like I'd been kicked by a Mississippi mule.

chapter fifteen

Snoop Dogg—inmate #A713J5-822, Long Beac City Jail.

chapter fifteen

i was busted, bagged, and popped, set up and knocked down, dead-to-rights and red-handed. The beef was possession with intent, and there was no fucking way I could cop a plea. They had all the evidence they needed, held on tight in my sweaty hand. I was going down and that was that.

Of course, in my line of work, a nigger gets used to being gaffled by the pigs. It was what you call an occupational hazard, and I'd had all kinds of minor shit on my record ever since I was in grade school. That's just the way it is in the ghetto. White youngbloods go to summer camp, play soccer, and cruise the mall. Black youngbloods break and enter, jack ghetto sleds, and broady whatever's not nailed down. Is it any wonder that half the brothers on the street have served time or are on parole in any given 'hood in America? We've got a criminal tradition that comes straight from the slave ships to the streets over a few hundred years of poverty and racism.

But I'm not about to get political on the situation. The plain fact was, I had a choice just like anybody else, and when I got hauled off and packed away, it was nothing I didn't know might happen if I kept selling rock long enough. I couldn't even blame those white motherfucking college kids for ratting me out. No way they were going to tell their rich mommy and daddy they'd been caught with their hands in the crack jar. Better to let some ghetto nigger take the fall and forget about the whole thing. You can take it from Snoop Dogg—you get in the way of the wheels of justice and they're going to flatten your ass.

Just like they flattened mine. When I saw all that steel pointing down my throat I knew I could kiss my hopes of being a rapper goodbye. Wherever I was heading with 213, it was history now. From that point on, my number wasn't going to be the fucking L.A. area code. It was going to be an inmate ID stamped on the pocket of my country blues.

The whole operation was nothing more that some bullshit politician trying to justify his existence by proving he was tough on crime. It's a regular occurrence in 'hoods across the country—some city councilman or D.A. or dog catcher is running tight for reelection and calls out the heat to make a sweep of the streets and boost the rap-sheet numbers before the vote gets counted. Every dealer and crackhead on the street has got to pay for this asshole's career, even though his clean sweep doesn't amount to anything more than putting a bunch of lower-level operators out of commission and making room for the next crop of mules and clockers. They never get anywhere near the heavyweights, because those niggers have got the cheese to buy their way clear up front. Like I said, you start hearing some City Hall suit talking about "making the streets safe for our children," you better get ghost and stay that way still the smoke clears.

As fast as all that shit came down on my head, that was as fast as I got moved through the courts. Check it out: once they got you and can add your name to their bottom line, they just seem to lose interest in making you pay for your crime. They've got no place to warehouse you anyway, and no room on the court calendar to give you a fair trial . . . or even a decent hearing. When you get caught up in the system, you get to feeling like a pawn in a big game of chess where you don't understand the rules, can't follow the action, and don't even know who's playing the game. You just get pushed around the board until someone wins and someone loses. And guess who does the losing.

They had me down in the city facility for the first couple of weeks after they brought me in, like they were trying to figure out what to do with me, and, in one regard, going back inside was no big deal. It was more or less like coming back to a home that didn't have a whole lot going for it except the advantage of familiarity. You knew where everything was, they had a place set out for you and the homies on the block were the same ones you used to marinate with back on the street. The only difference was, the cage you were in got a lot smaller from the ghetto to the cell block.

But in another regard, being back behind bars took something out of my spirit, like someone had pulled a plug and let all my hopes and dreams drain out the bottom. Before, I had gotten to the sorry place in my life that made jail seem like as good a place as any, since there really was no place I belonged and nowhere I really needed to be. But now, I had a goal I was going for. I wanted to rap and take my talent as far as I could, and the motherfucking block was nothing more than a giant step backward, one-eighty away from what I was working so hard to get. Right at the moment when things were finally going my way, my whole game got eighty-sixed and I was back where I started. Worse, I was back in jail, facing hard time.

After cold-cooling it in City, they brought me up to the county jail, which was a big step down the ladder, just as far as being able to keep your shit together from one hour to the next. County was full to the brim with all kinds of crazy motherfuckers and hardcore gangbangers who'd been knocked around the system for months or even years waiting for their court date to come up. All that shit about your right to a speedy trial has got nothing whatsoever to do with the reality of the situation inside. The courts are so clogged and there's so many cases backed up waiting for their day that you can easily get lost in the paperwork and shuffling back and forth and the delays and postponements and all the bullshit that goes on that, no matter how bad you want to jet, you've got to learn the virtue of patience or you're guaranteed to go out of your fucking skull.

Now, I've never been in a particular hurry about anything, but those first couple of weeks in County was about as much as I could stand and still keep my cool. Being inside this time was like a slow torture. I wanted out so bad and I would have given anything just to be with G and Nate back in the shed laying down some freestyle and blowing janky ganja.

Well, almost anything. I must have been on the block about two weeks when word came down through that the D.A.'s office was ready to deal. I got the news from my public defender, and you can't blame me for wondering if I was getting the best legal representation available when the motherfucker couldn't even remember my name from one meeting to another.

Anyway, the deal was a plea bargain: I'd cop to felony possession and they'd let me serve two years with time off for good behavior. Now, sitting around on that cell block twenty-four seven probably didn't do my state of mind much good, so by the time that offer rolled in I was feeling mean and dirty and about as ready as I'd ever been to cap any motherfucker who looked at me cross-eyed. My lawyer didn't have that problem. The fact is, the look he was giving me was like he was trying to remember which one of his seven hundred cases I was, but that was all I needed. I told him to tell the D.A., the mayor, and the chief of police to get in line and kiss my black ass one cheek at a time and then come back around and do it all over again. There was no way I was going to serve two fucking years, even *with* good behavior. I had things to do, places to go, and niggers to see, and that's what I told anyone who would listen.

Problem was, nobody was paying much attention. I spent another week cooling my heels, trying hard to get blunted on that skanky jailhouse weed all the *cholos* try to peddle. When my P.D. finally came back, I was more in the mood to deal, but this wasn't just because I was tired of wasting my time locked up.

It was probably about three days after I turned down that two-year deal when I got a call that there was a visitor waiting for me. As I made my way down the hall, passing one block after another and all of them looking exactly the same with trustees sweeping the floors and niggers' laundry hanging from the bars, I wondered who had bothered to come all the way downtown to look at my sorry face. That's one of the lethal side effects of being on the inside—you get to feeling like everyone outside has forgotten you ever existed, like you disappeared over the ocean in a plane and ended up on a desert island, never to be seen again.

I half expected G or Nate to be on the other side of the glass with the phone in his hand, telling me they'd just gotten a big record deal and were really sorry but they were going to have to move on without me, but that I could for sure get a free ticket to their concert next time they toured L.A. I guess I was feeling pretty sorry for myself, right about then, but that was nothing compared to the sorrow that rushed up over me when I saw who it was who'd come to pay me a visit.

I hadn't seen my mama more than a handful of times since she'd kicked me out of the house, and whenever I'd thought about her since then, I was quick to push her picture into a dark corner in my mind where I wouldn't have to face what had come between us. I knew she knew what was up with me ever since I'd hit the streets—the 'hood is too small to keep many secrets, especially between one family member and another. I wasn't sure she was on to how I'd used her place to run a secondary dope spot, but I got the feeling it wouldn't have mattered all that much even if she had. The bottom line was, I had broken her heart, and once the damage was done there wasn't much I could do to make it worse.

But my mama didn't come to scold me or tell me how I'd fucked up my life and thrown away my opportunities. She hadn't even come to cry over my sorry-ass situation. She was there for a whole other reason, a reason that, even today, brings out a tear when I remember it.

"Snoop," she said to me, her big dark eyes looking through my soul like she looked through the glass that kept us apart. "When I heard what happened, I wanted to come right down, find out if there was anything you needed, any way I could help. But, son, I realized there was nothing I could do for you anymore."

Her eyes filled up, but she shook her head like she was mad at herself for letting her emotions show, and she pushed back the tears and straightened up her back, never breaking her stare at me. "You're a man now," she said, "even though, to me, you'll always be my little Snoop." She was talking slow but steady, as if she were afraid that the words would stop altogether unless she forced them out, one after the other, in a straight line from her to me. "You've got to act like a man and take your punishment like a man." Now it was my turn to try and keep from crying. Right about then I felt like anything *but* a man, and all I wanted to do was to break through that glass and fall into her arms like it was back in the day and there was nothing safer or warmer than my mama's hug.

She kept on talking, even though her voice was so low I could barely hear it over the phone. "But I want you to know, son, that no matter what happens, what you do or what they do to you, I love you. I always will. Nothing can change that." She stopped then and just kept looking at me, like she was seeing her little boy underneath the grown-up skin that had covered him over. She got up to leave and it took everything inside me not to cry out after her to stay, not to leave me, that I needed nothing worse than to be her little boy again.

I stayed in that booth for a long time after Mama had gone, thinking about everything that had brought me up to this moment. I'd never seen the whole picture of my life, from beginning up to the latest chapter, in quite that way before. It was like I was counting backward to the day when it all started to go wrong and the longer I counted the farther back I went until I was just a youngblood again believing the best, without ever knowing what was in store for me. That's the sad thing about innocence. You never realize that you've got it until you lose it. And then you can never get it back. I'd made so many mistakes, turned down so many blind alleys, and there was no guarantee that it was ever going to be any different.

It was right about then that I shook myself and looked around and realized for the first time that I was alone in the visiting room. Everyone had split and the guard was taking a nap, his chair tilted back against the wall. It was the first time I'd been by myself, completely and totally, for about as long as I could remember, and in the silence that was around me, I could sense somebody, or something, sharing that space with me, filling up the air, breathing in and out in my lungs, keeping my heart beating and my blood flowing in my veins. I didn't hear a voice. No vision came through the bars of the window on a cloud of glory. But I sure enough realized, right then and there, that no matter what had come before, no matter what I'd done wrong, who I'd hurt and what price I had to pay . . . I still had a chance. A new beginning. Another day. I could make a difference in my life. I could make a difference in my mama's life. I could turn away from this place, and the life that had brought me here, and do something that had never been done before. It was now or never, and *never* had a final ring to it that sent a chill through my bones. Whatever else might happen to Snoop Dogg from that moment on, it wasn't ever going to be accidental again. I was awake, alive, on target, and on purpose. Today really *was* going to be the first day of the rest of my life, or I was going to die trying.

Maybe you could say I had some kind of religious experience, like when I was a kid in church and the preacher would get the poor sinners to come down front and ask Jesus into their hearts. Except I wasn't in church, there was no preacher, and I wasn't hearing any organ pumping away. It all happened in the quietness between my ears, between me and God, with no one else getting in the way. You can call that religion if you want, just don't start any Church of Snoop Dogg if you're looking for something to believe in. What happened to me was for *me* and for me alone. What the rest of you niggers do is on you. I'm just telling you the way it went down in my life because, like I said at the very beginning of this book, I'm about the truth. And this was my moment of truth, my fork in the road, my hour of destiny. And I grabbed onto it like I wanted to grab onto my mama.

And I'll tell you this while I'm at it. I know God looked into my heart and saw that I was sincere, that I was going for what He had with everything that was in me. I know because He gave me a sign to show that it was so.

When I got back to my cell that afternoon there was a message from my P.D. He'd gone back to the D.A. with the kiss-my-ass message that I'd given him. I guess they could have locked me up for good right then and there and then thrown away the key, just to show me who was boss.

But they didn't. By the grace of almighty God they made me another offer instead. I could plead guilty to a lesser charge—simple possession—and serve a year, half that with good behavior.

I sat on the edge of my bunk for a long time, just staring at the words on that piece of paper. I could do six months. I could do it sitting down. But, right then, I wasn't thinking about the time I had to serve. I was already on to the day I'd be free, not just free in body, but free in mind and spirit. Free indeed. That was the day that would make everything that came before it worth the wait.

chapter sixteen

Snoop Dogg, getting deep.

chapter sixteen

i can't say I exactly strolled through those six months—actually, the final count was six months and five days—but, like they say in the joint, you can do hard time or you can do easy time, and for me it was easy enough. I kept my nose clean, stayed out of gaffles, and dedicated myself to writing raps and perfecting my style. When I stopped to think on it, the hours just seemed to crawl by, with no end in sight. So I made it my business not to think about it, and sometimes a whole day would go by without me hardly noticing.

G and Nate would come and see me whenever they got a chance and it was a relief to me to find out that they had pretty much put 213 on hold until I got out. It made me realize that, as much as our group was a partnership, they knew up front they weren't going to get anywhere without me and were hanging back until I could get my skills into play.

I had a different feeling about the situation, although I was careful to keep it to myself. I never considered my homeboys as being essential to getting where I wanted to go as a rapper. Don't get me wrong—their encouragement and enthusiasm counted for a lot. But when it came down to ability, they just didn't have the same kind of natural talent that I was bringing to the game. Does that sound like I'm bragging on myself? I guess I am, but it's got to be better to admit up front what's true and what isn't than to pretend that we're all equal with nothing different between one nigger and another. That's pure bullshit. Everybody's got something they can do better than most people and you've got to acknowledge that if you want to take your talent to the next level. At the same time, you get on some motherfucking head trip about it, you give yourself just as much of a handicap. Don't think more of yourself, or less of yourself, than what you deserve, and remember—whatever it is you do, you can do it better than someone and someone can do it better than you. That keeps it real, all around.

For G and Nate, 213 was the bomb . . . like if we could make a record together we'd always have something to look back on and tell our grandkids about. For me, the group was a means to an end. I've always believed that it's important to have your homies around you at all times, just to remind you to keep it honest and stay in touch with the street. But when it comes down to it, rap is about one man using his skills to tell his story, his way. Two or three niggers on the mic at any given time may make for some interesting combinations, but it's a solitary voice, speaking from his own point of view, about what matters to him, that's made rap the most popular form of music on the planet today. Bust this—there's some phat cuzzes out there laying down crazy rhymes in combination. But it's the solo motherfucker who's got the goods, because when it all comes down, rap is nothing more than a man, his words, and the way he lays them out. At least that's the way I see it.

But, naturally, I didn't let on to my homeskillets that, one way or another, with them or without them, I was going to make my move in music. At that time, it was all for one and one for all, and as long as one of us was out of commission, then nothing was shaking for the rest of the crew. But we kept tight anyway because what we had between us wasn't just about where we wanted to go together, it was about where we'd been together and what we had in common.

I don't have to tell you that when the day came for me to walk out of County, looking fresh, dipped in threads my mama had brought down just for the occasion, it was like I'd been reborn into the world and was ready to make my presence known. I still had some ducats stashed away from my days with the Six One, enough to keep myself going until I could find a real job and get the 213 back up and running. I wasn't exactly sure what my first move was going to be, but I knew for sure what it *wasn't* going to be—I was finished with dealing rock. The whole fucking game was a scam. Big cheese, free pussy, gats, and gangsta style—and then they put your ass away for the duration. The game wasn't worth the ante, and even though I'm sure God doesn't let anything happen by accident, I also knew that, if I didn't take this lesson seriously, the next time I wouldn't be getting off so easy.

But it's funny how God works His game. Just when you think you've got Him figured out, some blindside twist of fate makes you understand that you *can't* figure Him out. That's why He's God and you're whoever the hell you are. He calls the shots, makes the moves, and keeps it all in check. You're just along for the ride.

The way I figure it is this: I was dead serious about changing my life. I knew I'd turned a corner back in that visitor's booth in County and there was nothing that could knock me off track. That's what I told myself, anyway. But what a nigger tells himself and what's the truth may be two entirely different things. Talk is cheap. What you back your rap with is what counts. And the way you know it counts is when you get tested. All the big plans and major moves you're going for don't mean shit unless they've been tried out in real life, just to see whether you can hang on to what you want, face down the obstacles and opposition that get thrown your way, and see it through to the end. God isn't interested in any chickenheads on His team. He's looking for those who can prove their talk by the way they walk.

And that was a lesson I was about to learn the hard way. Finally getting out of County was one of the happiest days of my life, except for one small problem. When you're inside, especially if it's only for a short count, you get to where you let down your guard a little bit and maybe don't take as good care of yourself as you did on the outside. It's no lie when they tell you that if the guards and the inmates don't kill you, the food will, and most cons eat as little of that slop as they can and instead get to depend on the care packages they get sent from their people. And what you can usually count on when you get one of those boxes at mail call is a batch of your mama's famous double chocolate chip cookies, or your auntie's pecan pie, or maybe just a big pile of your favorite candy bars. It's like they think all you'd ever be interested in is eating dessert, because, word, sweets is the favorite part of most people's diets to begin with and they figure sending you candy, cake, and cookies is going to make you feel better about being locked up.

For some niggers, maybe it does, but they're sure going to pay a price, eating all that shit and then sitting on their ass most of the day, watching their gut get bigger while they're scarfing down their favorite treats. The fact is, since they cut back on gym equipment and workout time in the joint, prison inmates are about the unhealthiest mother-fuckers around. It's hard to find anyone that's on swo like he used to be. You could call it one of the hidden punishments you get for having to go to jail in the first place.

I tried to take good care of myself when I was doing my time, but it wasn't easy, especially with my mama sending me boxes of Chips Ahoy and bags of Jolly Ranchers and all that other shit I used to steal from the liquor store when I was a kid. I didn't end up fat, but that's just because I'm so skinny to begin with, it doesn't matter *what* I eat—I never put on any poundage. But all that sugar sure enough did a number on my teeth, and the day I walked off my cell block, I had an ache in my back lower molar that was pounding like a bass speaker in a Benzi. I could feel the pain shooting all the way down to my bozack with every step I took, and my first move was to do a buck fifty down to the local dentist and get my grille taken care of.

There was nothing much left of that tooth to fill, so the man just yanked it out of my head and passed me over a script for codeine to take care of the ache I was sure to feel when the novocaine wore off. I didn't think twice about it as I headed over to G's crib where I was going to lay up for a few days until I could get my game together, and sure enough, after a couple of hours I could feel the throb starting to set in. I popped a couple of those pills and they did their trick. A half hour later I was feeling no pain, and right about then, everything I'd been though in the last twenty-four hours—from getting sprung to sitting in a dentist's chair to coming back to the 'hood for the first time since I made my choice to start a new life—it all caught up with me. I was dead on my feet and those downers the doctor had thrown my way just put me right over the edge. I was sound asleep by the time the streetlights outside G's windows lit up down the boulevard.

I can't tell you how long I was passed out. It could have been six minutes or six hours. All I knew for sure was that when I was shaken awake and opened my eyes to a bright light shining in my face, it took me a few seconds to realize I wasn't back on the block. By the time I remembered where I was, the pigs had already rousted me up off the couch and were hustling me out the door. I could hear G asking questions off in the background somewhere, but it seemed like he was in another room or even out of the window and down the street with his voice all quivery and echoing.

Whatever he was asking, the cops weren't answering, and it wasn't until we got down to the precinct house that I found out what their beef was. I'd been so focused on trying to get my grille taken care of, that I'd forgotten to report in to my parole officer. That alone was enough to send me back to the joint, but what happened next really sealed the deal.

I must have been acting a little bent-headed off that codeine, sitting in the cop house waiting to talk to my probation officer, because as soon as he showed up and took a look at my big black saucer eyes, he hauled my ass into a back room for an on-the-spot drug test. Needless to say, with all that script floating through my blood and piss I might as well have been a full-on cold-lamping junkie as far as they were concerned. Check it: I was in direct violation of the terms of my parole and I hadn't even been out of the joint for twelve motherfucking hours. That was the shit and I had no plea to cop, because nobody was listening, anyway.

I'll tell you something, free of charge. You face down a situation like that, you've got two choices—you can get bitter, or you can get better. And as far as Snoop Dogg went, *better* just wasn't an option. Damn straight I was bitter, walking back down that cell block with all those niggers in their cells whooping and hollering and telling me they'd been keeping my bunk warm for me, and me looking through the bars at the same tired scene I'd been staring at for six slow months and five slower days. Now I was back and I was mad at myself, mad at the pigs, mad at that dentist, but maddest of all at God. How could He do this to me? It was like He'd set me up just to watch me fall, like He was getting some kind of sadistic pleasure out of killing my hopes and dreams once and for all.

If, during my first stretch, I was determined to do easy time, now I didn't give a fuck whether it was hard *or* easy. And with that kind of attitude, you can believe I did some hard time. Breaking parole set me back another year to basically finish out my original sentence. That meant that, if I kept my nose clean, I could be out in another six months, but none of the arithmetic mattered much to me right about then. I was keyed up way tight and looking for someone, anyone, to take out my frustration on.

Before, I guess I was so wrapped up in starting something new in my life that I really didn't notice all the tension and fear that was leaking through the blocks around that time. This was back in the day before there had been a truce called between the Crips and Bloods, so you had this running gang warfare going on all around you, along with the regular racial gaffles between Mexicans and whites, whites and blacks, Samoans and Vietnamese and any other combination you'd care to pick from column A and column B. What had passed me by before was right in my face this time, and I was just waiting for someone to cross over my imaginary line in the dust, talk some shit about one of my homies, or dis the Crips. I was ready and willing to do some business upside any motherfucker's head. Someone was going to pay for the fact of me being back inside, and I didn't much care who it was going to be.

I figure the county authorities must have looked at my case and realized I was a bomb waiting to go off, because right away they put me on a work detail so I could blow off some of the heat that was building up inside. Basically, the drill was that they'd put you in the laundry, or the kitchen, or scrubbing toilets and it was just like any other job—you had to show up for work every day, on time and in line, or suffer the consequences.

Not that I cared much for the consequences. I was suffering for shit that wasn't even my fault, and if I was going to have to take any more punishment, you could be damn sure I was going to be deserving it this time.

In the case of County, the consequences were doled out at Sergeant's Court, which is where they'd send you if you missed out on your work detail for more than a couple of days running. They could add more time to your sentence, lock you down, or put your ass on the Nickel Crew, which was where I seemed to end up most of the time.

The Nickel Crew was where they'd send you out to a rock quarry, give you a hammer and chisel, and set you to busting up rocks bigger than you were for seven hours a day. There we'd be, just like in the movies, a bunch of convicts breaking up boulders in the hot sun. The only things missing were those pajama-stripe uniforms and the big ball on a chain around your ankle. The fact was, the situation out in that quarry was about the loosest in the whole system when it came to security, and you had motherfuckers escaping there on a regular basis.

I'm just thankful that I never got it into my skull to break out. The truth is, I think it was all the time I spent on the Nickel Crew that really got me through my second stretch without trying to bust some insane move. It was like I could take out all my aggression on those big old rocks, breaking them down smaller and smaller like I was trying to break down the pieces of my anger until I could grind it to dust underneath my heel.

And it worked. By the end of the day, I'd be so tired and sweaty, about all I could do was hit the showers and turn in, most of the time a good couple of hours before lights out. I can't say I felt a whole lot better for all that chiseling and hammering I was doing—every night when my head hit the pillow I'd still be asking myself how I got into the mess I was in—but somehow the days passed on, one after another, like inmates in a roll-call line shouting out down the row.

After four solid months of working, sleeping, and listening to wheels turning in my mind, I got the news that they were fixing to spring me early. Maybe they thought I'd gotten a raw deal to begin with and were trying to make it up to me. But I don't think so. Most likely they had to make room for someone else and needed my bunk space. I wasn't complaining, and even if my mood going out the second time wasn't anywhere near as happy and carefree as when I'd last walked out those doors, I was sure of one thing. Make that two.

First, I was never going back.

Second, I'd be watching how much candy I ate from then on.

Me and my Gs: (top)
Fred Dogg, (bottom, left
to right) Joe Cool, and
Nate Dread.

chapter seventeen

Right about here, I've got to take a deep breath and slow down a step to figure out where I've been and where I go from here. This book game is brand new to me, and writing out the story of my life, using words that don't rhyme to tell a story from beginning to end, brings up lots of memories you'd forgotten all about and gets you thinking about the turns your life has taken while you weren't even noticing. And it's about here in the story that the plot begins to go in a whole different direction.

I don't know about you, but for Snoop Dogg there have been certain special moments that, looking back, have broken my flow in half. I'm going along with one beat, strong and solid, and suddenly the tempo changes, the pace picks up, and you've got to move to a new rhythm or get left behind. For verse after verse, you're freestyling like a champ and everything's coming easy. Then, from out of nowhere, you're dealing with facts and factors, circumstances and situations that are strange and unfamiliar, with a whole different perspective that you haven't got the vocabulary to describe.

That's what it was like when I walked out of jail for the last time. All around me, everything looked just like it had when I went in, and if you'd asked me then, I couldn't have told you for sure that anything special had changed. But it had. It's like everything up to that point had been a preparation for everything else that was coming afterward.

Let me put it this way: looking back on everything that's happened to me so far, I'd have to say my story isn't all that different from a lot of other niggers' in Long Beach, California, or, for that matter, any other ghetto 'hood from one coast to the next. My father was gone, my mother working to hold the family together; I started out in life dreaming about a slice of the American pie, being a sports star or a music celebrity, before the hard truths of racism and poverty caught up with me; trouble in school, trouble at home, trouble on the streets; gangs and drugs and jail; then more gangs and drugs and jail; then one more black child flushed down the toilet of a system that just don't give a shit. It's the same sad story, heard a hundred thousand times, twenty-four seven, as every day of the week we get one step closer to Judgment Day.

Except, for this particular nigger, it didn't end up like it usually does—a toe-tagged DOA in the country morgue, capped in a drive-by or OD'd in some alley with a crack pipe stuck in his mouth, or clocked by AIDS or any other of too many ways to die in this day and age. Something different happened to Snoop Dogg, something like a miracle or divine intervention or fate or destiny or whatever the fuck you care to call it. All I know is that suddenly my life had a purpose. To increase the peace. To spread the music. To educate and elevate.

I can't say it happened right away, like one morning I just opened my eyes and the world was a different place. But there's no doubt in my mind that by getting around and through everything that had been put up in my way, I had proven myself worthy to carry out God's calling. And when He finally moved on me, He didn't waste any time.

The year was 1991, the season was late spring, heating up into early summer, that time when the 'hood starts to stir and niggers get into a party mood. Of course, I didn't exactly have a lot to get jiggy about right then. More than anything else, it felt like I was right back where I started from, just a year older, and only some bumps and bruises to show for everything I'd been through. I was broke, I was unemployed, and I was an ex-con. Strike three—your ass is out. True enough, Shanté stuck by me, Auntie Mary was there to give me a kick in the ass when I needed it, and my mama made it clear I always had a place with her.

G and Nate were sticking tight, but the fact was, coming up on twenty years old, I had shit to show for myself.

Except for one thing—determination. I can't even tell you what I was so determined about, except that I knew, no matter what, I wasn't going back to selling drugs or trying to be a player in the gangsta game. I was over that shit. And, as far as rap went . . . well, I didn't know *where* it went, or how to track it down. My dream of making a name for myself in the music business seemed further away than ever and I had exactly nothing to show for all the work I'd put into developing my talent up to then.

Almost nothing, that is. What I did have was my style, polished and perfected during those long sessions with 213 in the toolshed and by myself on the block after a day on the Nickel Crew, with nothing to do but run rhymes through my brain. Without hardly even knowing it, I was learning my craft, taking my music to the next level, and getting myself together even when all it looked like a waste of time. I'd gotten to a place where my confidence was based on experience, knowledge, and discipline. I was ready for the world. The question was, was the world ready for me?

Not so that you'd notice. No major label, big-time manager, or hot-shit producer was banging down the door looking for the next big thing out of Long Beach, which left me to take my place in line with about a million other motherfuckers all trying to get themselves no-ticed. The only edge I brought to the game was that I was good. Fuck, I was great. I knew it and everyone who heard me knew it. Now, it was just a matter of waiting, hoping, and working hard.

Which is what I did. The waiting and hoping came natural, it was the hard work that took a little getting used to. After all, I'd been pulling down phat bank for a couple of years in the Six One crew and now I was going to have to support my ass on minimum wage while at the same time spending every spare minute trying to get my music on tape and out to the right ears. It was like working two full-time jobs for a tenth of the cheese I was used to.

But I wasn't complaining. Anything was better than being on the in-side of a cell, watching yourself get slowly toasted like raw hamburger in a microwave. I got my ass in gear, taking a job as a box boy at a little mom-and-pop grocery store on Atlantic not far from my old 'hood and, after hours and on weekends, clocking some solid time with G, putting together demo tapes.

By this time, the future of 213 was way up in the air. Nate was starting to do his own thing and G was more or less committed to helping me get my game off the ground. Like I said before, the nigger is my main man, there for me through thick and thin . . . and the other way around, too. Even when I was still in the joint, he'd scouted around and found a funky little four-track studio setup in back of a place called V.I.P. Records, a local store run by a righteous homey by the name of Kelvin Anderson.

Kelvin was like a lot of brothers in the 'hood, working a half dozen games at the same time in hopes that one of them would pay off sooner or later. First up, he had his record store, one of the best in the 'hood and one of the few places that actually served the community. The L.B. ghetto wasn't exactly the kind of place Virgin Megastore or any of those other big chains were shoving each other aside to get into, so it was down to cats like Kelvin to meet the needs on the street as best they could.

Along with the store, Kelvin had his little label, V.I.P. Records, where he'd give a shot to local talent whenever he could, pressing up records and selling them mostly out of his own place. He managed a couple of brothers, had a publishing company, and, aside from all that, maintained a janky little recording studio in the back of the stockroom at V.I.P.

World-class nagger that he was, G got on Kelvin's back and wouldn't jump off until he got some free time in that studio for us to do our thing. We spent most afternoons in there, and as many nights as we could spare, with me taking over the rap spot and G doing most of the mixing and producing. Kelvin had gotten hold of a beat-to-shit drum machine that G got down cold, milking every last sound he could out of that piece of junk and running it through that four-track backward and forward until he came up with the beat that matched whatever it was that was going on between his ears.

For my part, the raps I was laying down were finally starting to talk about what was real in my world. Thanks to N.W.A and some other niggers out of Compton, it felt like there was space opening up to talk about conditions on the street, what homies' lives were really like and how gangs and drugs and violence had become part of our everyday routine of survival. I can't say I moved in that direction on purpose, like I was deliberately trying to piss people off or call attention to myself by getting on the mic and laying it out like I saw going down around me. That was what I knew, goddamnit, and right about that point in my life I had a lot to say about the way things were and how they got that way. I wasn't looking for controversy, publicity, or notoriety—I was looking to get out what I had inside, and I honestly didn't give a fuck whether anyone was offended or not. I was going to do this my way or not at all . . .

All through that summer and fall we stayed holed up in Kelvin's back room, working our game and getting it tighter and more together with each session. G had started putting together some tapes of our shit, picking out our best numbers and running them together on cassettes until we had four or five in a row that we could righteously be proud of.

After that, things really started moving. Kelvin took to spending more and more time back in the studio with us, sometimes making suggestions, but most of the time just sitting there soaking in the sounds we were coming up with. I liked Kelvin. He was an older brother, but he knew what was what and my guess is that, at least in the beginning, he was letting us use his facilities because it would keep us off the street and out of trouble. But it didn't take him too long to realize we were onto something dope, and he made an offer to take one of our demos around to his record-company contacts.

That was cool with us, even though we weren't sure Kelvin's connections were going to do us a whole lot of good. If he was so hooked up, what was he doing running a low-down record store in the middle of the ghetto, anyway? But we let him do his thang and kept our fingers crossed.

The way I saw it, Kelvin might just be our only way to someone in the music industry who could help us move off the dime. I'd given up on even considering G's half brother, Dr. Dre, a long time ago. After all, we'd sent him a batch of our stuff, and while he gave it a fair hearing for the sake of his family tie with G, all we ever heard back was that we needed to keep working on our chops. I just figured that was the polite way of telling us we didn't have what it took, so I never got on G's ass to get back to Dre with new tapes. I figured we'd already burned that bridge behind us.

But G saw it a little differently. One thing about the nigger, he's tenacious as a pit bull with rabies, and once he gets his teeth into something he just never lets it go. And in the case of Dre, he wasn't about to let that connection slide. Never mind that G had a family call on his half brother—by this time the Doctor was the hottest producer, songwriter, and recording star in rap music, hands down. He'd had an incredible run with N.W.A on tracks like "Dopeman" and "8 Ball," and when he and Yella and Eazy-E started producing acts for Ruthless Records, they scored big with J. J. Fad and some other up-and-comers. Then came Above the Law, with their *Livin' Like Hustlers* album, D.O.C.'s *No One Can Do It Better,* and two more N.W.A platinum sellers, *100 Miles and Runnin'* and *Efil4zaggin,* all of them with the unmistakable Dre sound busting out all over. Anywhere you'd read his name, they'd be talking about "the godfather of gangsta rap," and, for my money, it was Dre more than any other nigger who put the West Coast on the rap map. Even after N.W.A broke apart and Dre and Eazy got deep into their shit, he was still top dog on the scene. A little company called Death Row Records would one day prove that point beyond a doubt.

So, like I said, while I was figuring Dre had better things to do than listen to our homemade demos, G was bound and determined to get his foot back in the door. Kelvin was trying his best, but was coming up zero, so, from G's point of view, he didn't have anything to lose by slipping our demo into Dre's party basket, in hopes he'd play it one night.

It was only after the fact that I heard what happened when that tape came up in rotation during a stag party Dre was throwing out at his mansion. A couple of minutes into the first cut, everybody had stopped what they were doing to listen. A couple of minutes later they were dancing, and by the end of the track they were shouting for more. G got a call the next day that Dre wanted to see him and the skinny-ass rapper who he'd been working with.

That first meeting I had with the Doctor was up at Death Row's brand-new office in Hollywood, and I'd be lying if I didn't tell you I was nervous as hell. Like every other nigger in America, just about all

I'd been listening to for the past year was music that Dre had either written, produced, recorded, or performed, and it felt like being in the presence of a superstar to be ushered through the lobby by the superfly receptionist and back into the big corner office where Dre did his business. I couldn't help thinking that this was a long ways from where I was used to being, the other side of the world from the mean streets of Long Beach.

But, after a few minutes hanging with Dre, I got to feeling more comfortable. G and him were tight, and I could see that, for all his money and influence, he was still in touch with the streets and what was going down outside his penthouse office. We hadn't talked for too long, just bullshitting about nothing in particular, when Dre leaned over his desk and asked me to give him a sample of my freestyle.

I got nervous all over again, but managed to spin out a decent flow, riffing on how Dre was number one and bringing up the names of all his records and the artists he'd worked with just to let him know that I was on top of his game. When I was done, Dre had a big smile on his face and turned to G.

"You all come down to the studio tomorrow morning at eight o'clock," he said. "I got something I'd like to use you on."

"That might be a problem," G said, and I could hardly believe my ears. What was this nigger talking about? "We had to take a bus out here today," G continued, smooth as silk. "For us to get to the studio at eight, we'd have to get our asses out of bed at six in the morning. We ain't gonna be exactly fresh by the time we get there."

Dre just gave him a long look and I swear he didn't blink once. Then he busted out laughing and, picking up the phone, hit the automatic dial.

"We got some guests coming out to the house tonight," he said to whoever was on the other end of the line. "You make sure you treat them right, understand?"

He hung up and turned back to us. "Now, you niggers are about to see how the other half lives," he said. "You better get used to it, too. Because you stick with me and you both be going places."

chapter eighteen

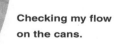

Checking my flow
on the cans.

chapter eighteen

the first place we went was up to Dre's, out in some superwhite part of town with Lexuses and Benzies and Beemers parked along a windy canyon road. When we showed up, it seemed like there'd been a twenty-four-hour-a-day party going on up there for the last couple of months, with homies and fine bitches just draped all over the leather furniture or kicking it naked-style out by the pool where the outdoor speakers were blasting Dre's music out across the whole valley like the trumpet call of the four fucking horsemen or something.

G and I tried to stay cool and keep our jaws from dropping open every time some beautiful bizzo would come walking by with her booty hanging out, or some brothers would bring us into a huddle around a bong full of primo ganja, but it was hard to pretend that our funky ghetto minds weren't blown by the high styling and profiling going down at Dre's pad. Maybe some other nigger would have gotten himself motivated by all that scrilla, and get to asking himself how he could get in on the action, but for Snoop Dogg, it was way intimidating, like Dre was the daddy and all these homeboys and girls were his little children, holding out their hands for the goodies he could give out. It seemed like being a player like Dre was a lot of responsibility, and I found myself wondering what it all had to do with making music. That was something I'd find out sooner than I expected.

We hung out there all night, smoking weed and watching porno on Dre's wall-to-wall TV, and it was about two in the morning when I wandered off to find someplace to sack out. I wanted to be as fresh as I could for the next morning, hoping that if we did a good enough job with whatever Dre had in mind, we might catch the break we'd been looking for.

I got up next morning bright and early to the smell of bacon, eggs, and indo drifting through the house. Dre was sitting in the kitchen in a gym suit, watching his cook get breakfast together for a couple dozen sleepy-eyed party peeps, who'd either just crawled out of the covers or had never gotten to sleep in the first place. I took a seat next to him and gave him my biggest smile, just to let him know I was primed and ready for action. But he just looked at me with bloodshot eyes and groaned. It didn't look to me like he was ready for anything.

Right about then, the phone rang, and for the next ten minutes Dre did his best to cool out some situation that sounded way out of hand. After he hung up, he told me what was what: he'd been hired to write some music for a movie called *Deep Cover* and he was supposed to be down at the studio right then to cut the track. The only problem was, he didn't have it ready; in fact, he hadn't even written it yet. And that was where I came in.

"We got about an hour and a half before we gotta be cutting this motherfucker," Dre said. "So I tell you what: I'm going to the gym for a workout. Meanwhile you put something down for me." He stood up and started heading for the door.

"Hold a minute," I shouted after him. "What's this song supposed to be *about*?"

"That's up to you," he said. "But I'll give you the first line if you want it."

"Yeah," I answered, trying to keep the sarcasm out of my voice. "That might help."

Dre smiled. "Start it out with 'Tonight's the night I get in some shit / Deep cover on the incognito trip.'" I couldn't tell whether he had just made those lines up off the top of his head, or whether he'd worked them out beforehand. Not that it much mattered—he was out the door before I had a chance to ask him where the rap was supposed to go from there, and when I asked G, he just shrugged and told me, "It's like he said—that's up to you."

So for the next hour I sat at the breakfast table, smoking Dre's chronic, eating a plateful of bacon and eggs, and scribbling out any lines I could think of. At first I didn't have a clue where I was going, but after a couple of dead-end tries I came up with a plan. "Tonight's the night I get in some shit" reminded me of the night *I* got into some shit, so I decided to write a rap about my bust. I've got to say, under the circumstances, what with the clock ticking and so much at stake, it was one of my better efforts, and I felt pretty good about what I'd come up with when Dre got back and I handed him the scrawled-out piece of paper.

He was still all hot and sweaty from his workout, but he stood in the hallway and read the whole thing through and when he was done he looked up at me, as matter-of-fact as you please, and said, "This is the shit. We got us a hit."

I could hardly believe my ears. It was all so simple . . . except that I had been working for years to get to this moment. Everything I'd ever learned about rap music, about making every word count and keeping it real, had gone into putting down "Deep Cover." You could say that, all of sudden, I was about to be an overnight success. Or you could look at it another way: all the hard work, disappointments, and determination that it took to get me this far had finally paid off. But, to tell you the truth, I didn't much care what way it came down. Dre was telling me I had a hit, and from that motherfucker's mouth, the words sure enough meant something.

We all piled into Dre's 300SL and jammed down to the studio where a bass player Dre had hired was cooling out, waiting for the session to start. G and Dre got together on a drum machine and laid out a rhythm track, then the bassist, a brother named Colin Wolfe—one talented homey I'd be getting to know real well—tried out one riff after another until he found something the Doctor was happy with. The next step was to lay in the vocal track, with me and Dre trading lines, and that was that.

Night was just about falling by the time we finished the session and headed out down the 405 back to Long Beach. It felt like we'd done a good day's work, and if anyone had asked me where I thought "Deep

Cover" was going I'd have told them straight to the top, just based on how hyped Dre was on the track. But the truth is, I would have had my fingers crossed while I was saying it. I liked what we'd done, but it didn't sound any better or worse than a dozen other rap hits on the radio at that time. I couldn't have told you for sure whether we'd gotten something special out of that session or if Dre was just bullshitting us, trying to impress a couple of L.B. niggers out on the wrong side of town.

The truth was, I had as much an idea about how you get a hit record as I did about how to drop science on astrophysics or some such shit. It took me a long time to figure out that the most important ingredient in selling records is momentum. And that's what Dr. Dre had, big time.

Don't get me wrong. "Deep Cover" was a good track. We'd put down a phat drum-and-bass riff and my rap had all the right street attitude that was coming into its own right about then. Dre and me made a good pairing on the vocals, each playing off the other's phrasing and giving our lines a twist that hooked them together without the seams showing. But the reality was, there was plenty of great music coming correct all around us: looking back, I'd say the early nineties was the golden age of gangsta rap. You couldn't walk down a street in America without hearing some hype beat come booming out of someone's ride. What was going to make our little cut stand out and be noticed?

The answer was the big M. Momentum. Dre was the hottest of the hot rap producers going, and "Deep Cover" came along at just the right time to take his career as a performer right over the top. The kind of attention it called down just feeds on itself until you've got a media frenzy that pulls everybody into its orbit.

Like I said, things were moving quick, even though you couldn't tell from outward appearances. Even while "Deep Cover" was starting to shoot up the charts, and it seemed like everywhere I went I could hear my own voice rapping out that refrain, "187 murder on an undercover cop," my lifestyle hadn't changed all that much and I sure as hell wasn't living like Dre. The fact was, I didn't have a permanent address to speak of and from night to night could be found at G's or Dre's, Mary's or my mama's, sacked out in a spare room or on a foldout sofa. Shanté and I were keeping regular around then, but we weren't drinking Remy at any five-star joint in Beverly Hills or any of that fine shit. We were satisfied going to McDonald's and a movie whenever we had a spare night, which, as that year went on, got to be harder and harder to come by.

Dre had recognized right away that "Deep Cover" was no fluke, that if I could write a hit that quick, imagine what I could do with a little time to stretch out and strut my stuff? He put me to work right away, writing, freestyling, and putting it all down in the studio, good, bad, or any other way he could get it. That was the way Dre worked—he sucked it all in, let it digest awhile, and used it for fuel to fire up his own creative flow. He was as much a collector and collaborator as he was a solo attraction, but what he added to whatever you were doing, you just couldn't get anywhere else. The magic touch, a gold thumb—you can call it what you want, Dre made it happen.

Of course, music wasn't the only thing happening around Dre and his posse at that time. His battle with Eazy-E over the profits from Ruthless Records was turning nastier by the day, and when he hooked up with a big, bearish former football pro turned record executive named Suge Knight, the lines between legitimate business and straight-up gang warfare got real fuzzy. Dre was in the middle of it all, making threats and filing lawsuits and generally keeping his name in the papers by matching his music-making abilities with his troublemaking abilities. Looking back, I have to say that Dre was, without question, the hypest talent in rap music at the time. My only regret for the brother is that he wasted so much of that time fighting the same old turf battles that made the 'hood such a dangerous place to be. It's like he just transferred that whole mentality into the recording studio and the record-label offices, when all along he should have been doing what he does best: making great rap records.

I say that all that because, to this day, I know he and I are tight as any homies can be. We've been through too much together, good and bad, to ever let politics or business get in the way of our friendship. All the same, though, the shit that was surrounding him at that time made it harder for me to get where I was going. I had to step carefully to stay out of his way and keep myself focused on the music. And that wasn't always so easy.

But, word: that's just my way of seeing things. Maybe one day Dre will write his own fucking book and it will all come out different. I'm giving you one side of the story and there's always two sides to everything. At least. All I can say is, I tried to keep my name and my nose out of the hardcore tactics that Suge and his crew at Death Row would use to get what they wanted. I was always proud to be part of a record label that was as successful and influential as Death Row, from a creative point of view. But when it came to extortion and assault and hanging people out of windows to get them to sign over their publishing . . . that kind of shit I'd just stay the fuck away from. I'd done my time as a gangsta. Now I was about being a rapper, first, foremost, and finally. And there was no question, regardless of what else he was involved with, that Dre was helping me get to where I wanted to be, on the fast track. I'll always be grateful to him for giving me a chance to prove myself.

For a while there, Dre had been working up an idea for what you might call a concept album, a kind of gangsta's manifesto about the hardcore truths of the ghetto from the point of view of the niggers that were down there living it out, one day at a time. But he wasn't so much coming at it from a political viewpoint—Ice-T and other motherfuckers had that covered already. In his mind, the project was more about a state of mind, a way of seeing the world and what it meant to get by on your wits, your reputation, and your survival skills. Of course, any time you start delving into life as it's really lived on the streets, you're going to touch a raw nerve. Racism, poverty, violence, addiction . . . those are facts of ghetto life. But what Dre saw was something else behind all the statistics—niggers standing up to be counted, taking a risk to tell the truth, and letting the words stand on their own, no explanation or justification needed.

When he found Snoop Dogg, I think he found the perfect spark plug to get those creative cylinders firing. I was like a fresh reminder to him of where he'd come from and what the niggers from Compton to C-Town to Chocolate City had on their minds. In the fall of 1991, even while "Deep Cover" was still going strong, Dre and I started meeting regularly, sometimes just the two of us, sometimes with Colin Wolfe or top rappers like RBX and D.O.C., and started throwing rhymes around, trading ideas and trying to hone in on a point of view that could carry through a whole album. At one point, my old homey Nate Dogg showed up to add some verses to a rap he'd written originally back for 213 called "Deeez Nuuuts." We were one big happy family, and as the work went on, I could see that it was D.O.C. who was really pushing Dre to put his best into the project. He believed in what we were doing, and sometimes I think it was that belief that kept us going when times got rough and the flows weren't happening the way Dre wanted. D.O.C. was about it from jump and we all owe him for that.

We kept at it, adding and taking away, building up and tearing down, until something special started to take shape. By the time we got into the studio to begin laying it down, we all knew we were sitting on the bomb album of the decade, which only made the tension run higher as we put together the bed tracks. We all had a stake it bringing this motherfucker off right and it was like we felt a personal responsibility to Dre to give it the best we had. Speaking for myself, I knew that even if the album wasn't going to come out under my name, Dre had given me enough space on the tracks to push me over the top if I did my job right and delivered what he was after.

But looking back on those sessions, I've got to say that the Doctor never seemed to lose confidence in me or any of the other rappers and musicians he put together to help him pull it off. And by the time we were finished, that list was a who's who of up-and-coming rap stars. Aside from me and G, Nate, and D.O.C., Dre had pulled Kurupt, Dat Nigga Daz, one of his own discoveries named Jewell, and about three dozen other players who were all jammed into that sound booth at any one time.

It was during those long hours in the studio that I learned the fine art of making a record, straight from the master. Dre always kept it cool and loose, never gave anybody cause to think they weren't wanted or needed, and, most important of all, kept a steady supply of the finest indo rolling in from sunup to sundown.

Considering how much ganja got blown in that studio, it shouldn't have come as a surprise to anyone that, when Dr. Dre's album finally hit the streets, the artwork featured a big old green cannabis leaf and Dre's head in place of the Zig-Zag man on a pack of rolling papers. The name of the album? What else—*The Chronic.*

chapter nineteen

Snoop Dogg in full effe

chapter nineteen

nd the rest is history. That's most times how they describe what happens when you get to this part of the story. But, for my money, it isn't what happens next that's history—it's everything that happened up to that moment, when your life suddenly becomes public property, you're living in a media fishbowl, and privacy is something you give up without even knowing you're losing it.

Check it out. Being famous isn't about finally starting to live your life the way you always imagined it was going to be. It's about living some other life entirely, one where the old rules don't apply, friends become strangers, and everything you thought you could depend on gets lost in a superstar shuffle. Getting to the top and staying sane on the way up is about the toughest game you can play. You've got to keep your wits sharp, twenty-four seven, or you're going to find out real quick what they mean when they say "It's lonely at the top." It's all too easy to get yourself isolated, live behind a big wall in a gated, guarded mansion on a hill, surround yourself with motherfuckers whose only job is to say *yes* to everything you want, and all you can think about is that big pile of money you're sitting on and that maybe, just because you're paranoid, it doesn't mean someone's not trailing your ass, waiting for an opportunity to take it all away.

To me, being famous is kind of like being in jail, and you can either serve your time the hard way or the easy way. It took me a while to figure out how to tell the difference between the two.

Of course, the success of *The Chronic* was history making, no question about that. Dre had taken his lifelong love of George Clinton, Parliament, and the Funkadelic posse, and updated it for a new generation, and the result was the biggest-selling rap album of that time, clocking in sales of more than five million before all was said and done. Writers and critics were talking about how we'd revolutionized the appeal of rap music right across the barriers and races and generations, and while maybe that was all just a bunch of media hype, there was no doubt that a lot of people, black and white, young and old, were picking up what we were laying down. "Nuthin' but a 'G' Thang" became kind of an anthem for kids, and no matter where you went, it seemed like you were hearing "Bow-wow-wow, yippie-yo, yippie-yay" being chanted like the theme song for youngbloods of every description.

It had taken a long time for gangsta rap to work its way up from the black underground—from Schoolly D, Public Enemy, and Boogie Down Productions, right up through N.W.A, Ice-T, and Ice Cube. But it was *The Chronic* that busted it wide open and it was Dre and the rest of us who took most of the heat for celebrating the gangbanger lifestyle in our music. *Chronic* cuts like "The Day the Niggaz Took Over," "The $20 Sack Pyramid," and "Stranded on Death Row" didn't say anything that hadn't been said in Schoolly's "Saturday Night," Public Enemy's "You're Gonna Get Yours," or KRS-One's "9mm Goes Bang"—we just said it so the whole world could hear and suddenly we were front and center, taking the flak for telling the truth about life on the streets.

Politicians and educators and civic leaders and anybody who thought their opinion counted for something were pointing at us and shouting that we were part of the problem and that our music was like pouring gasoline on a fire that was going to set the ghetto ablaze. It was like, all of a sudden, the whole world had woken up to the violence and despair that was all around them and had to find someone to blame for a situation that was out of control. And like it always happens, the first motherfucker who gets his finger pointed at him is the one who breaks the bad news.

I'm not about to tell you with a straight face that *The Chronic* didn't incite some niggers, somewhere, to try out the "'G' Thang" for themselves. You put out your music because that's what comes from your heart and soul. What happens once it's out there is anybody's guess, and everybody's responsibility. But I will say this, straight up: *The Chronic* gave a lot of disenfranchised brothers, black *and* white, a voice to say the things that needed saying. We were telling it like it was, not like it should be or even could be, but the actual, stone-cold facts, straight from the 'hood and into the suburban living rooms of America. No wonder that record freaked people out.

At the same time, *The Chronic* forced a choice on me right away. I was going to be a spokesperson, whether I liked it or not, and what I had to decide was who I was speaking for. Right up front, Dre had recognized my talent as an asset for *his* career, and it was no mistake that he had put me front and center on the video for "Deep Cover." It was his music behind my raps—even the hook from "Nuthin' but a 'G' Thang" was a riff he'd borrowed from his hero George Clinton on the track "Atomic Dog"—and whatever credit, or blame, got parceled out, it went to him first before any of it trickled down to me. When "'G' Thang" got nominated for a Grammy that year, for instance, Dre was the one who got all the juice, and that's the way it should have been—it was his record, with his picture on the cover and his name on the credits.

But if I was going to hitch a ride on Dre's sled, I needed to know right up front that he and I were tracking. And to tell you the truth, some of the shit the Doctor had gotten himself in, with all that controversy about Ruthless and the way he and Suge Knight were muscling their way into the music business, made me realize I had to keep my distance. The last thing I wanted was to get caught up in *their* shit. I needed to concentrate on what I did best—rapping—and the whole situation was putting my bozack in a vise. I mean, there I was, a key player on the hottest record in the history of rap, my words being heard from coast to coast and my face popping up in heavy rotation on MTV, but as far as most people knew, I was just Dre's sidekick. When the brother spoke, he was speaking for me. And what he said was supposed to be what I meant. I didn't have a clear shot at making my own way, not as long as I was just another nigger in the Doctor's stable. I found myself starting to hang back a little, biding my time until I could make my move and trying to keep my own momentum going without getting too close to Dre's heat. It was the first time I really had to play the celebrity game, knowing when to be out front and when to fade into the wallpaper. But it wasn't going to be the last time.

The Chronic just kept on moving up the charts, topping the rap and R&B lists before crossing over to pop and peaking at number two. All in all that album would hang in on the charts for more than eight months. We'd milk the ride for a couple of more hit singles, including "Dre Day" and "Let Me Ride," but even while the album was still hitting strong I was laying plans to make my own move.

I had to be careful. The last thing I wanted to do was get on the wrong side of Dre or Suge, especially since the two of them had their own label, Death Row Records, up and running. The fact was, I *needed* Dre, and not just because he was the heaviest-weight contender in music at that time, but because he was also the best fucking rap producer working out there. Period.

Of course, that street went two ways. Anybody who'd paid any attention knew that I was behind the phattest tracks on *The Chronic* and that the reality was, even though I'd hadn't had so much as a single put out under my own name, I was, all in, the rapper everyone was talking about. Whatever Dre's next move would be, he was going to have to deal with me, one way or the other.

All throughout '92, I'd been writing reams of rap lyrics, trying to keep on top of my game while at the same time meeting Dre's demand for more and more material. Dre was spreading himself pretty thin, as far as I was concerned. Aside from working on his own shit, he was writing and producing for a bunch of other acts including Tha Dogg Pound, a group that featured Kurupt and a cousin of mine out of Long Beach named Daz. I guess Dre must have been thinking that rap talent runs in the blood and he wanted to get everyone in my family that he could find hooked up, just to see if they had the same skills as me. Daz wasn't bad for a youngblood, and I did what I could to help him along. The same goes for my homeskillet G, who didn't make it a secret how he felt that Dre had moved him out and taken over the territory. Whenever I got the opportunity, I would tip the press to my main man, hoping some of the spotlight that was falling on me would leak over on to him.

Most of the time, though, I was too busy to do much of anything but write, rap, and try to keep my game plan in order. Sometimes it felt to me like I was working two jobs, building my own career and at the same time keeping Dre's moving along, and right away I knew I had to make myself a promise and keep to it: no one was going to get my best material but me. Snoop Dogg, the rapper, was the first and only nigger who could do justice to Snoop Dogg, the writer, and no matter what kind of grand strategy Dre had for my stuff, I held back the prime raps, ready for the day when I could record them myself.

That day finally came late in the year, when Dre and Suge finally got their distribution deal together for Death Row with Interscope Records and announced to the world that one of their first releases was going to be my solo debut album. Finally, I was going to get my props. And maybe a little cheese along with it.

You'd think that after the run we'd had with *The Chronic,* everyone involved would have enough juice to never worry again. But that wasn't the way it came down. While I can't tell you exactly what happened to all the proceeds from that album, I do know that none of us niggers were getting rich off of it. I remember Nate telling me how he had to do a little street business just to get enough cash to buy gas for trips to the recording studio, and while I wasn't exactly that hard up, my personal scrilla wasn't in a whole lot better shape. I could excuse the situation given the fact that *The Chronic* was really Dre's album, regardless of how much he had lifted from the rest of us to make it work, but there weren't going to be any excuses when it came to anything that had *my* name on it. Snoop Dogg was going to get *paid,* and that was that.

As it turned out, once we got rolling on the album, that payday started to look further and further away. Now, anyone who's worked with the brother will tell you that Dr. Dre is one meticulous producer. He knows what he wants and he won't be satisfied until he gets it, no matter how long that may take. And, in the case of my album, it was a motherfucking marathon. His typical approach would be to pick a song, do six or eight or ten takes of it, then start editing down the best segments from each take. That slicing and dicing might go on for hours and it might go on for days, but no matter how much time and energy he put into it, if the final result didn't meet up to his expectation, he'd throw it away and start the process all over again. When some writer asked him why it was taking so long to get my album out, Dre was quoted as saying that the tracks he was doing for me were "the future of funk." "I never heard of a perfect hip-hop album," he went on, "but I'd like to make one."

Don't get me wrong: I wanted my album to be the best it could be, just as much as Dre did. But I had some legitimate concerns, and up at the top of that list was that I wanted to be young enough to still enjoy my success when it came around. It had been well over a year since he'd released *The Chronic,* and I was starting to wonder if people would still remember who I was or, worse, if some upstart nigger would grab my style and run with it, all while Dre was laying low in the studio making the "perfect hip-hop album."

Actually, make that studio*s*. We must have spent time in a dozen different places all across L.A., from Village Recorder to TRAX to The Complex to Larrabee North *and* West, including long hours at Dre's own home rig, over the months it was taking to get that album in shape. And most of the time, when we had to move, it didn't have anything to do with trying to find a better sound or more up-to-date equipment. The fact was, the posse Dre had invited by sometimes got so out of hand that we were invited to leave and take our bongs and cases of Coqui 900 and out-of-hand bitches along with us.

And it wasn't just the nonstop partying that got in the way of work, either. On more than one occasion, Suge Knight would show and try to put his two cents into the mix, and while we all respected what he was doing business-wise, he didn't know as much as he thought he did when it came to making a record. That, in itself, could have been dealt with: you listen to the motherfucker, wait until he leaves, then do exactly what you were going to do in the first place. But Suge insisted on adding his own gangsta prejudices to the mix. See, the brother had Blood affiliations, and more often than not, the crew that would come down with him to the studio were some hardcore Blood bangers. To say that the situation created some tensions with the Crips that were *our* friends is to put it mildly. Sometimes we'd have to call a halt to the recording session because a fight had broken out in the booth, with Suge in the middle getting everyone worked up and taking sides, one against the other.

So, in the end, was it all worth it? Hey, you listen to *Doggystyle,* even now, coming up on seven years after it first came out, and tell me you don't think Dre got about as close to the perfect hip-hop sound as anyone ever has.

Throughout the whole process of making that record, as fucked up and crazy as things around us were getting, I had one, and only one, major goal: to keep the music real. This was going to be my shot at opening up my life to the rest of the world, to get across my point of view and reflect what the truth on the streets—not just the problems, but the way we handled what came our way—was really all about. There was no way I would let anything stop me from going for broke. After we finally got the album in the can, for instance, some art director from the record company came around with a bunch of jive mock-ups of what they wanted the cover to be. I told them then, and I kept telling them until they heard me, that I already *knew* what the cover was going to be. I had another cousin who'd just gotten out of the joint, Darryl Daniel, who we called Joe Cool, a good cartoonist who could make something of his talent if he could just get a break. I passed the job on to him, and what he delivered was exactly what I wanted—a rude and lewd comic strip that made me laugh out loud every time I looked at it. I might have given Dre as much room as he needed to do his thing with the music, but now that the album was done, and my name was going on the cover, I was going to take it from here. And if they didn't like it . . . well, you know the rest.

Which brings us back to where we started this chapter, about the rest being history and all that. Even before the record hit the streets, Dre and I had been on the covers of *Vibe, The Source,* and *Rolling Stone,* and the week *Doggystyle* was released it hit number one on the *Billboard* charts, the first time *that* had ever happened for a solo artist with a debut album. We came on strong with the single "Who Am I (What's My Name)?" and followed that up with "Gin and Juice" and "Doggy Dogg World," and it seemed like every time a new track hit the airwaves, the album would go shooting back up the charts. Before it was all over, we'd sell six million copies of *Doggystyle* around the world, and Snoop Dogg would become a household name.

You'd think my troubles would have been over. But they hadn't even really begun.

chapter twenty

Taking aim in the movie
Hotboys.

chapter twenty

Let me give you a little idea of the action that flamed up around *Doggystyle* even before the record hit the streets. The scene was the rooftop of V.I.P. Records, where I'd been posing for hours as part of the video shoot for the album's first single, "Who Am I (What's My Name)?" You know the one, where I morph into a Doberman pinscher? I thought so.

Anyway, it's eight in the morning and me and the crew had been at it pretty much since dawn. The idea of getting started so early was to avoid the crowds of curious bystanders that get attracted to a film set like flies to shit. We had it in mind to get in, get our shots done, and move on before the 'hood even woke up.

But it wasn't turning out that way. Somehow, word of our arrival had spread around town the night before, so by the time dawn cracked over the hills behind L.A., the street was already clogged with a thousand motherfuckers, drinking forty-ouncers and pulling on king-size blunts before they'd even had breakfast. We barely got our shots in before the crowd started surging past the police lines and shoving their way to the front of the store, trying to get a look at me. It was strange and, straight up, a little bit scary to see so many faces I recognized from growing up on these streets coming at me like they wanted to either worship me or sacrifice me. We got out of there just as some of those niggers had started to scale the walls and made our way up a couple of blocks to King Park, where the next shot was scheduled.

By the time we showed up, the scene in the park was even more crazy than on the street. As I tried to make my way up to where the scene was going to be shot—a peaceful picnic all laid out on the grass and set to be overrun with Dobermans—we could see bangers wearing their full colors coming up from every direction. Suge had insisted early on I get myself a bodyguard, and even though I didn't see the need exactly, I found a beefy brother from Iowa named McKinley "Malik" Lee who I liked and trusted to do the job. And right about then I was sure glad he was covering my ass, especially when one mean son of a bitch sidled up alongside me and started talking about how I thought I was hot shit and it was going to be up to the brothers to cut me down to size and a bunch of other hardcore threats that I didn't quite catch because all I really was paying attention to was the mad-dog look in this nigger's eyes. I'd never seen anything like it—a mix of jealousy and hatred and some kind of killer instinct that had come up against me not because of anything I'd done, but just because I was who I was: Snoop Doggy Dogg, rap star, media figure, and public fucking property.

As Malik hustled the guy off, I heard a sound coming up fast like the wail of a wounded elephant and looked up to see a fleet of ghetto birds coming in so low you could read the police serial numbers on their underbellies. Pigs were leaning out the doors with bullhorns, shouting for everyone to disperse, and from somewhere in the crowd I heard the sudden rapid-fire popping of a semiautomatic. Half the crowd hit the grass while the other half set off on a rampage, overturning trash cans, breaking car windows, and spilling out onto the street looking for something else to burn, break, or bust open. A line of cops in riot gear started moving across King Park, sweeping up the mob in front of them and driving the whole packed mass right toward us. I turned and looked at Dre, who'd been standing beside me the whole time. In a split second we both scoped out the situation and realized there was no way to get out from under that crazed herd.

Then, just when it looked like we were going to get our asses totally trampled, this little white Mercedes comes tearing across the field, throwing up dust and dirt and clumps of grass. The car swerves to a stop in front of us, the back door opens, and two hands reach out and pull us both in. It was Suge Knight to the rescue.

Having lived through experiences like that, it was easy to believe what I was reading every day in the newspapers and magazines and hearing all the time on the radio and TV—that *Doggystyle* was a certified cultural phenomenon, that the music had tapped into the new voice of a generation, that Snoop Doggy Dogg was the first real superstar in the realm of rap, and a bunch of other bullshit that seemed like it was both too hyped up to be real and not nearly strong enough to describe what was really going on out there.

Whatever had been happening to me before did not, in any way, prepare me for what was happening now. Rap music had been waiting to break out in a big way for a long while now, and it took me being in the right place with the right music at the right time to blow the roof off the motherfucker. *Doggystyle* was more than a hit album—it was the national fucking anthem of the Republic of Rap. Snoop Dogg had arrived and anyone that needed proof just had to stick his head out his front door and listen. My music was everywhere.

And so was I. In the days and weeks after we finally got *Doggystyle* out to the people, it seems like I was turning down more interviews than I was taking, sifting through the offers that came pouring into the Death Row offices and picking out only the cream of the crop. At first, I was right on the one with my schedule, making sure to show up on time and in order to give them the quotes and the photos and the face time they wanted to make their magazine or TV show look good.

But it didn't take too long to realize who was really running the game when it came to PR. When you're first starting out, maybe you need all the exposure you can get, and you get it by cultivating anyone who can give you a little ink or a few seconds of air time, like *they* were the one doing *you* a favor.

But the reality is, they aren't going to have a magazine or a newspaper or a TV show if they can't get to you, and if you got the brains and the balls to control your access and call your own shots, then you'll have the press eating out of your hand instead of the other way around.

There are two expressions I've heard that apply directly to getting famous and staying that way. One is, nothing succeeds like success. Once you reach a certain point, get yourself far enough out front and make a big enough splash, the interest, the attention, and the demand will feed on themselves. Then it's just a question of how much you feel like going along with the game. I took to showing up an hour, two hours, three hours late for some interview or photo session and came to find out that, the later I came, the happier they were to see me. Shit, sometimes I just didn't bother showing up at all and they'd be on the phone bright and early next morning trying to reschedule. When you're top Dogg, they play by your rules.

But there's also another side to that game, another expression that describes just what it's like to be the focus of all that love and worship and acclaim, twenty-four seven, no matter where you go: be careful what you wish for; it might just come true. I would have to be stupid not to read the spray paint on the wall after shit like the King Park incident went down. It was clear as mud that, whatever my life once might have been, it wasn't going to be like that anymore. Whatever I might have been missing before, when I was just another poor nigger on the streets of Long Beach, at least I could still show my face in public without having to call out the fucking SWAT team. I could go where I wanted, when I wanted, with whoever I wanted, and stay as long as I wanted. Now I had to fight for the right to my own time and space. Privacy was a thing of the past. Like it or not, I was up front and on display, night and day, from the time I got up in the morning to the time I finally got to close my weary eyes at night.

And it wasn't just my old way of living that I had to kiss goodbye. Now that I was Snoop Doggy Dogg, gangsta supreme, I became a target for anyone who had something to get off their chest. On the one side, the guardians of American morality were getting upside my head about the violence and sexism and drug use that I was supposed to be advocating in my music. Those motherfuckers I could deal with—it was a free country and I could say whatever I wanted, just like the millions of fans who bought my records could listen if they wanted to. Words by themselves never killed anybody—not my words, and not the words of those high and mighty house niggers who tried to stifle my music.

But bullets can kill you, and what had me worried was the fact that, because of my high profile, I was a sitting duck for the ongoing turf war between the Crips and the Bloods. That riot in the park was nothing to the fear I felt when we started shooting another video, this time for "Gin and Juice," out in a Compton 'hood that was a Blood stronghold and a crew showed up flashing red bandannas and baseball bats. It was like my success was counted on the Crip side of the ledger, and until some Blood made it like I had, there was going to be a score that needed settling. Like it or not, my past was following me into my future, breathing hard down my neck.

It was for that reason that I made the decision to get out of Long Beach and move to a place where I didn't feel like I was sitting in the crosshairs all the time. Now, I've heard a lot of niggers get down on me for picking up and moving away from my roots, and my answer to them is straight up and simple: fuck y'all. You don't know what it's like trying to maintain a regular lifestyle when you've got the most famous face in the country and everybody and their mother is on your ass to hear their demo, spot them some cheese, or blow your head off because you got something they don't.

I got no sympathy for all those white motherfuckers living up in their triple-gated fortresses because they're too paranoid to try and make it in the real world. But I *lived* in the real world my whole damn life, and when it's time to go for the sake of yourself and your family, you better do the right thing or you *deserve* what comes down on your ass.

So we relocated—me and my mama and my brothers and Shanté. I made sure all of us were safe and secure and well looked after, and I don't have to explain that to anybody. That's what a man does when he's got responsibilities, and if you wouldn't do the same, then you're stupider than the assholes that tried to call me out for deserting the 'hood and all the rest of that shit. Hell, it wasn't like I was some white pop star singing about spooning under the June moon. I'm a motherfucking gangsta rapper, the best there is, and the words I rhyme with are real. They come straight out of my experience, and in my experience, it's real easy to get killed once you start calling attention to yourself. I'm about survival for me and mine, and if that means picking up and moving behind the biggest, highest wall they can build, you can bet your ass I'll be there, and writing out a big fat check to pay for it, too.

Which is exactly what I did when I moved everybody out to a beautiful new home in an exclusive 'hood up in L.A. And if you still don't think I had a good enough reason to leave, I'll give you one more.

It happened one night a week or so before *Doggystyle* hit the streets and Shanté and I were kicking back at her place late one night after I'd managed to grab a few hours for myself to spend with her. Ever since I'd showed up at the door, dropped off in Suge's limo, I could tell she had something on her mind—the way she hung back, kept to herself, and was even quieter than she normally is, all tipped me off that Shanté was deep into something, and knowing her, I figured she'd tell me when she was good and ready and not a moment before.

That moment came after the credits started to roll on the video we were watching and the grandfather clock in her hallway suddenly started sounding out the hour, loud and clear.

"Snoop," she asked me, in a voice so soft I could hardly hear her, "what do you think is gonna happen with us?"

"What do you mean, baby?" I answered, thinking she was talking about me getting famous and what it would mean to her. "You and I will always be tight. Nothing's going to change that."

My words seemed to satisfy her and she put her head on my shoulder for what seemed like a long time before she looked up again and said, "You think one day . . ." she stammered, then blushed, and I could see she was having a hard time getting to what she wanted to say, " . . . we might, you know . . . start a family or something?"

"Sure, baby," I said, thinking to myself that someday could be any day and that, when that time came around, I'd deal with it then. "Kids are the bomb . . . you know how I feel about youngbloods."

She smiled, the dimples getting deep in her cheeks. "I'm so glad to hear you say that," she said, and then there was a long pause while she waited for me to put it together.

Well, maybe I'm not too smart when it comes to that kind of stuff, because I just sat there smiling back like a Halloween pumpkin, tugging on a blunt and hoping that, sooner or later, she was going to get to the point.

I didn't have to wait long. She caught me with those big, brown eyes and held me in a stare, while out in the hallway, the grandfather clock ticked louder and louder. "Snoop," she said finally, when it was obvious I wasn't following her lead, "what if that day was now?"

I blinked. Then I blinked again. The blunt between my fingers went out, and through the door that damn clock sounded like a time bomb set to explode on my ass. "You mean . . . ?" I said finally, swallowing hard.

"That's right," she answered, with a serious look on her face I never quite remembered seeing before. "We're gonna have a baby, Snoop."

Now it was my beating heart that was sounding like time bomb. My mind raced, forward and backward at the same time, as I remembered the years I'd spent watching my little brother or our adopted homey, Martin, growing up, thinking back on all the diapers I'd changed and all the baby food I tried to get into their sloppy little mouths. Then I found myself thinking about what was to come, the hopes and dreams I had for tomorrow, the success that had come my way and that I hoped would still be happening for me years on. Trying to wrap my brain around all that at once made me kind of dizzy, and maybe I turned a little green because Shanté got a scared look on her face and asked me if I was feeling all right.

"I'm okay," I told her. "Just . . . give me a minute, baby." I sat back on the sofa and tried to put it together one more time. I didn't know where I was going, not exactly, but I did know that I didn't want to go there alone. And when I remembered being around the youngsters in my house growing up, it suddenly seemed to me like it was one of the happiest times of my life. Sure, having a baby was a big step, maybe the biggest step I'd ever taken. And that was because, no matter what, I would make sure that I was doing the right thing by that kid, being a father in a way that I'd never had a father—being there when it counted and coming through, one day at a time.

And I figured, if I already felt that way about it, maybe I was ready after all. Or maybe you're never ready, not exactly, but you find something in yourself when you have to that brings you to the place you've got to be, to do the right thing.

"I hope it's a boy," I said to Shanté, and leaned over to give the mother of my child a big wet kiss.

chapter twenty-one

The No Limit crew: (standing, left to right) Mystikal, C-Murder, Snoop, (seated, left to right) Mia X, Silkk the Shocker.

chapter twenty-one

'll bet everyone's asked themselves the question at one time or another in their lives, lying awake at night and chewing over the big topics, like the meaning of life, what we're here for, and what God's plan is for our time on earth. And somewhere down along the mental road you're walking you start to wondering what really matters and what's just the bullshit that gets thrown up to distract you. Have you made the right choices when you came up to them? Do you know what's real, or are you living in some dream of your own imagination? What's truth and what's a lie and how can you tell the difference?

And right about then you maybe think up a certain scenario that would clear up all those questions in a flash and you run it down to yourself: What if I was illing and I went to the doctor and he told me I had six months to live? Or six weeks? Or six days? What would I do with the time that was left to me? How could I make every minute count? Would I be able to tell what's right, what's real, and what's the truth, and would it even matter as I watched my life drain away like sand in one of those egg timers?

Then again, maybe not everybody asks questions to themselves like that. Maybe we're all just too busy trying to get by to ever look at the big picture and work out where we fit into it. Maybe it's just me that's been kept awake at night thinking on things like that, asking myself if what I was doing on a day-to-day basis added up to anything more than just simple survival. Maybe I'm strange that way. Maybe it's my blessing . . . or my curse.

But I don't think so. My guess is, we all wonder about the time we've got set out for us on the planet and what we're going to do with it before the clock stops ticking and they put us in the ground, say a few words, walk away, and forget we ever existed. But it could be that, for a few of us, the answer to those questions is a little bit more important than it is for the rest of us. And that might be because, for those few, the reality of their life coming to a stone-cold stop is more than just some what-if trick their minds play on them. Every once in a while, a human being, no different from you or me, really does face down those odds, and when that happens, nothing is ever the same again.

I know what the fuck I'm talking about. Because it happened to me.

And, when it did, it changed the way I came at every part of my life. You could hear it in my music; you could see it in the way I dealt with friends and family; you could pick up on it by the way I walked and talked, like I was carrying around one of those boulders we used to break up on the Nickel Crew, chained to my back and bearing down heavier with every step I took. I've stared death in the face every day, and not just that black hole you fall into when your time is up. Because there's worse things than that kind of dying. There's a living death that even today makes my blood run cold just thinking about it. It's called a Life Sentence Without Possibility of Parole.

Everything I'd built, everything I'd worked for, every connection I'd made to this world, was under threat of being cut off forever. I faced the reality of living out my days in a steel cell, watching myself get older one hour at a time, and waiting so long for that last hour to put me out of my misery that I'd actually look to death as a way to finally get free. And when you're living with that possibility, you start to see things in a different way. If you never prayed before, you learn how real quick. And if mercy was something you never thought you needed, or even deserved, you find out fast that all that is ever going to count for much is God's mercy on your poor, pitiful soul. You get grateful for the small things and count every blessing. Food tastes different. Breathing is a privilege. And every time you wake up free for one more day, you feel like crying and laughing at the same time. That's where I was at for three years, and that's why I am who I am today. What doesn't kill us makes us stronger. And since I just about went down to living death in a prison cell, that must make me one strong motherfucker.

But let me back up, take this thing from the beginning, and try my best to explain to you what really happened and maybe even take a shot at why it went down the way it did. There's already been a pile of shit written, talked about, and chewed over regarding certain events on the day of August 25, 1993, and most of it is nothing but pure speculation—the kind of lies people tell each other when they don't know the truth but want to say something anyway. This is the one version of the story you can believe, because I was there, I saw it all go down, and besides, I already told you . . . I don't lie.

We were still working on *Doggystyle* pretty much twenty-four seven at that time, trying to meet a record-company deadline that kept getting pushed back anyway, the deeper Dre got into his game. I'd already taken my first step toward moving out of Long Beach, renting an apartment out in the Palms district of L.A., a nice, quiet middle-class neighborhood that just happened to be alongside the border of one of the most notorious housing projects in the city, Nickerson Gardens. I was sharing the place with Daz at the time. My bodyguard, Malik, had taken the place next door with his wife and kid, and Death Row was picking up the tab for both cribs. I considered the whole thing a temporary setup, since the place was close by the studio we were working in at the time and besides, trying to bring that record in took up so much energy, I didn't much care what I was doing during my downtime so long as I could cool out in peace.

Every once in a while a homey from the old 'hood would drop by to get me up to speed on the latest Long Beach gossip or just hang around working the Playstation that the label had brought in to help me unwind at the end of a long session. That morning a nigger named Sean Abrams, a.k.a. Sean Dogg, who I'd been tight with ever since high school, called up wanting to come around. He hung out a lot back then, he and a handful of other 'bloods who liked being part of my orbit.

There was always food to eat, a six-pack in the fridge, and a pile of blunts rolled up on the coffee table, so for them, coming to see me was like a vacation. They had no idea the pressure I was under to keep my game moving in the right direction, and I didn't need to let them know. They were my guests, I was the host, and as long as my friends were under my roof I wanted to make sure they were enjoying themselves.

Daz and I rolled out of bed around noon that day, split a reefer, ate some Froot Loops, and played a couple of video games just to slide into the day before we had to get down to the studio. We couldn't have been at it more than an hour or so when I heard the sound of loud footsteps outside the door, like someone charging down the stairs. I turned to look at Daz, but neither one of us was freaked—not just then, anyway. News about me moving into that apartment had spread fast, and there was nothing special about fans coming up and leaving presents at the front door at all hours. I guess we both were figuring it to be something along those lines, when suddenly, out the window that looked over the street, we could hear voices shouting at each other.

Now, if you grow up in the ghetto you learn right away to tell the difference between niggers just messing with each other and some serious shit about to go down, and from the sound of things outside, something serious was getting under way. My instinct told me to stay away from the window, but I got up anyway and, moving over, peeked around the sill to see what was going on.

The first thing I noticed was a dark-colored Cordova, a real pimp-wagon, parked at the curb. I couldn't tell who was inside, but standing on the sidewalk was Sean Dogg, yelling and pointing to someone in the passenger seat. I could tell right away it wasn't a friendly discussion.

"What's goin' on, Snoop?" Daz asked behind me.

"Sit tight," I said. "Be cool. I'll be back in a minute." I headed for the front door with Daz's big eyes following me and went into the hallway. Standing across the way was Malik's wife, looking like she'd just seen Casper. She still had a bag of groceries in her hands and I immediately figured out it was her I'd heard charging up the stairs a minute before.

"What's going on, Tina?" I asked her and waited until she could stutter out the story: she'd gone out to do some shopping and when she got back Sean was standing in front of the building, having a full-on gaffle with three niggers in a car.

Three against one. I didn't like those odds. My best guess, based on past experience, was that these motherfuckers didn't have a beef with Sean Dogg. It was my face they wanted to get into, and I wasn't about to let my homey take on trouble that had come looking for me. I ran down the stairs two at a time to see Malik, my bodyguard, standing at the landing watching what was going down from the shadow of the doorway.

As soon as he caught sight of me, Malik pushed my ass back into the shadows. I didn't hold it against him. It was his job to protect me, and this was a situation that looked like it could get out of hand before you had time to think about it.

While I hung back, trying my best to see out the lobby into the bright sunshine, Malik began to walk slowly toward Sean and the carload of bangers. As my eyes adjusted to the light, I could see their faces in the car, all hyped up and twisted with rage. Two of them were complete strangers to me, but I thought I recognized the one in the backseat as a crazy nigger who, a while back, had actually drawn a gat on me during a video shoot at a gas station before he got hauled away by the security guards on the set. I didn't know his name then, but I sure enough would know it by the time that week let out: Philip Woldemariam.

In fact, I'd find out a lot more about Philip than just his name, a lot more than I really needed to know. The nigger was an immigrant from Ethiopia who'd come to America when he was still a youngster and gotten deep into gangbanging from jump. He'd been part of a crew called the By Yerself Hustlers, because they'd never been able to get hooked up with either the Crips or the Bloods and were working on an indie tip. At the time our paths crossed, he was serving one year's probation for shooting off a gun in public—just one more wild motherfucker looking to make a name for himself like some young punk gunslinger in Dodge City. Which I guess made me Marshal Dillon, at least in his mind.

I couldn't exactly tell from that distance what they were fighting about, but I could see the one in the front passenger seat throwing up his gang set in Sean's face and knew they must have been calling him out over turf, like he had dared to show his face in the wrong part of town. It was all just crazy, anyway—this was about Snoop Doggy Dogg and the bragging rights for anyone who could cut him down to size. Sean Dogg just happened to show up and now he was taking the heat, in the line of my fire.

I was just about to make a move onto the sidewalk, show my face and give him a chance to get out of the way, when Malik moved up next to the car to let himself be seen. The brother has got some bulk to him, for sure, and he's cut from all the pumping he does, so they knew right away this was no leg pull.

"Word, 'blood," he said, kind of under his breath so they had to shut up to hear him. "We ain't banging 'round here. You got the wrong niggers."

The By Yerself looked at each other. It was obvious that Malik evened the odds and it was time for them to rethink their game. The driver hit the pedal and the Cordova took off with a squeal of burning rubber.

Even as we were watching the car disappear around the corner, Malik had hustled Sean back into the lobby and, grabbing me by the arm, hauled us both upstairs and into the apartment. Once we were safe, he went back outside to make sure the car hadn't just circled around the block, and for the first time since the shit had started to go down, I let myself breathe.

Relief turned to anger, and it was hard to keep my feelings to myself. I couldn't understand why I was all of a sudden the target of every fucked-up player hater and janky overhyped banger who thought he had something to prove. I was about music, making people feel good and getting them up and dancing, but it wasn't enough just to try and bring something positive into the world. For some other people, it was about keeping everybody down at the same level, as if, since we had all come from the same place of poverty and ignorance and violence, we all had to stay there. Anybody who tried to raise his head above the crowd ran the risk of getting it chopped off.

I went on in that way for a good half-hour until Malik came back and reported that the coast was clear. By that time I'd calmed down enough to start getting my act together for the studio. It was about two o'clock and I think we were all pretty shaken up, but business was business and it was time to head out. Daz decided to stay behind, leaving Malik, Sean, and me on our own.

We didn't get very far, first because the Jeep Cherokee I'd just bought was about out of gas, and second because once we stopped at the station, Sean realized we'd left the tape of last night's session back at the apartment.

Since Malik didn't know the area as well as I did, I got behind the wheel and took us back to the corner of Woodbine and Vinton, where I started to park in front of my building. It was right about then that Malik, who was sitting up front in the passenger seat, nudged me in the elbow and pointed down the street, where we could see someone coming up to us fast on foot.

I recognized him immediately. It was the banger in the front seat of the Cordova who'd been throwing gang signs in Sean's face. My first thought was to just pull on around him and keep on driving, and I've heard it said that your first instinct is always your best instinct. Maybe if I'd followed it, this would be a whole different book, but I didn't, and it isn't, so this is what happened next.

The nigger, whose name I later found out was Jason London, flagged us down, and as I pulled to a stop I could see the driver of the

Cordova, Dushuan Joseph, sitting at a picnic table in a little park across the street. When he noticed that I noticed him, he stood up and opened up his shirt to show that he wasn't packing. At the same time, Malik was rolling down the window to hear what London was trying to say.

"We ain't sweatin' y'all," the nigger insisted as he approached the Cherokee. "It's just my homeboy Phil . . . he be trippin' sometimes, that's all."

And as soon as he said his name, the motherfucker appeared, like out of nowhere, bearing down hard on the car at full tilt. I froze at the wheel, not sure whether to back up, go straight on, or hit the floor and start praying. Woldemariam was coming up fast and I could catch a clear shot of something bulging out of the waistband of his pants. With the kind of street-level training I had coming up, I didn't have to look at it twice. If it was a gun, or if it wasn't a gun, I didn't care. I knew something bad was about to go down and all I could think of in the moment was that this was sure a fucked-up way to die, like a sitting duck, capped by a nigger I didn't even know.

Woldemariam came to a stop in front of the Jeep and London started talking to him, trying to cool him out. As if it were all happening in slow motion, I saw Malik pull out a nine-millimeter, load in a clip, and set it on his lap. The incredible thing was, Malik was no believer in firepower and had only borrowed the gat two days before from a friend because Suge had insisted he carry one for my protection.

I looked up from the gun, out beyond the windshield, to where Woldemariam had shoved London aside and stood alone, a little off the right side of us. I saw him spread his legs and crouch low, and I knew what that was about. He was bracing himself, getting in firing position. I closed my eyes and could hear a loud rushing between my ears, like a wind blowing through my skull. I felt a heavy blow in my stomach and bent over in sudden, harsh pain. The cab of the Jeep exploded in sound, so loud you couldn't think. Shots went off. *Bang. Bang. Bang. Bang. Bang.* Five times. The roaring in my ears was so loud it hurt. I opened my eyes, half expecting to see holes in my gut and my shirt starting to soak up blood.

But I was all right, and I realized that Malik had hit me in the stomach to get me to lean over and take me out of the line of fire.

In the next instant, my eyes took in about a dozen images, all at the same time.

Malik, beside me, the smoking gun in his hand.

Sean, in the backseat, crouched down and lying so still I didn't know whether he was dead or alive.

Outside the window, on the street, London and Joseph, standing stock still, like store-window dummies on display.

Between them, the crumpled body of Philip Woldemariam, heaped up like so much useless meat on the asphalt.

chapter
twenty-two

Showing my colors for
No Limit.

chapter twenty-two

and that's how it began, a nightmare that would take three years out of my life and remind me, each and every day, that I was living on borrowed time. No matter what else happened after that bloody afternoon on the peaceful streets of Palms—no matter how successful my career became, or how blessed I was by becoming a family man—there wasn't a minute that passed when I wasn't aware that it could all be taken away from me, that my future was not my own and that the hopes and dreams I'd reached for so long could be snatched out of my hand forever, at a moment's notice.

In a mess like I found myself in, you tend to freeze up, waiting for events to take their own course of action and hoping against hope that somehow it will all go away. But I've got to hand it to Suge Knight. He was on the case from jump, taking charge of the situation and coming at it from every angle he could think of, up to and including legality, publicity, and security.

His first move was to stash us someplace safe until he could get with his lawyers and map out a strategy, so we all got hustled over to the Beverly Garland Hotel and were told to lay low until we got a phone call from Suge or his lawyer, David Kenner.

It was in the penthouse suite that I first heard word of how the police were going to play the whole incident. The eleven o'clock news that night spelled it out in language anyone could understand: "Famed gangster rapper Snoop Doggy Dogg," the blow-dried anchorman reported, "his bodyguard McKinley Lee, and an accomplice, Sean Abrams, are suspects in a drive-by shooting in the Palms area of West Los Angeles." All the code words were there, if you knew how to read them—"gangster rapper," "accomplice," "suspects," "drive-by"—and no one had to tell me that the D.A. was ready to go to the wall with this one. After all, the public had been worked up into frenzy by the press about the so-called gang warfare epidemic breaking out all over the city, and now they had a convenient scapegoat to make an example of and show they were doing their job, like it says on the side of their wagons—To Protect and Serve. Like the O.J. trial that was still to come, high-profile defendants make for good headlines at reelection time. I was about to get thrown to the wolves.

Behind the scenes, Suge and Kenner were working hard to negotiate a safe surrender when the time came to turn ourselves in. We'd registered under fake names at the hotel and never left our rooms once during the three days we hung around waiting for the lawyers to work out details with the police. Nobody knew where we were and Suge made sure it stayed that way, just in case the cops tried to put pressure on our women. Thinking back, that was the hardest thing of all to put up with during those three endless days—I wanted so much to talk to Shanté, to tell her I was all right and that I didn't do what they were saying I had done. I needed her to know that I was taking our future together seriously and that I would never jeopardize it by getting in the middle of some fucking gang skirmish.

But I had other things on my mind, as well. I had been scheduled to appear as a presenter at the MTV awards at the Universal Amphitheater and I was bound and determined to make that date no matter what. It wasn't even so much about the award show itself—getting your face on TV for two minutes was no big deal to me, even then. But I settled it in my mind that I wasn't going to let the cops, or anyone else, run me to the ground at the exact time in my life when I should have been reaping some of the benefits of all my hard work. I was going to *go* to that motherfucking award show, no matter what.

The night of the broadcast, word came down that the cops were going show up backstage in force to take me away right after I did my thing, but even that didn't slow me down. I set it up through Suge to have a running car waiting out back for me and even planned my escape route beforehand. Then I made sure that I arrived at the hall with seconds to spare before I was supposed to go on.

I'll never forget stepping out onto that stage, with those blazing lights blinding me, and hearing thousands of voices calling out my name until the house was rocking on its foundations. I knew that, for every voice in that auditorium, there were ten thousand more across the country that felt the same way, and in that moment it was like I had a million homies standing shoulder to shoulder with me, ready to face whatever would come. I raised my hands high above my head, looked up to the heavens, and shouted as loud as I could, "I'm innocent!"

The place just came apart, and with the sound of cheering still ringing in my ears, I ducked out the back, into the idling car, and was halfway down the hill when I saw twenty cop cars, their cherries flashing and their sirens wailing, coming up the other side of the road.

The driver turned to me. "Where to, boss?" he asked.

I gave him the name of a restaurant close by where Suge had arranged for me to meet Kenner and, together, go to the police and turn myself in. I'd had my moment in the light. I'd made my statement for the whole world to hear. Let them do their worst. I was ready.

Kenner posted my million-dollar bail, as he'd arranged with the D.A. beforehand. Just like I figured, the charge was murder, with a parole violation thrown in for good measure. And at the pretrial hearing a few weeks later, I came back with a strong not guilty plea on both counts. This time around, there wasn't going to be a plea bargain, no deals and no time off for good behavior. I was down for the fight of my life and it was winner take all.

Of course, whoever it was that said the wheels of justice turn slowly knew exactly what the fuck he was talking about. After everything was said and done and all the suits had made their motions and entered their objections and stood on the courthouse steps talking in front of the microphones and cameras, I was given a trial date of November 30 and sent home to wait out my fate however I could find the strength and patience and faith to do it.

I'll tell you straight up, that was the hardest time I ever did—harder than any sentence I ever served in the joint, harder than all the time I sat waiting around on a corner to sell a dub rock to some crackwhore, harder than hoping that the world would discover what a great rapper I was. Like I said, what doesn't kill you makes you stronger. And that time, waiting to find out if I was headed for the joint for the rest of my life just about killed me.

You'd maybe think that with all the other shit going on around me, I wouldn't have been able to think about my date with destiny, and for some of the time, at least, that was true. After all, it was right about then that *Doggystyle* got released and racked up fifteen million dollars in sales its first two weeks out. Did the publicity around my murder charge help move that record out of the stores faster than pancakes at a church breakfast? You better believe it. I had what you'd call "instant credibility," and Suge and his team at Death Row used it for everything they could.

And on top of the incredible heat that was getting generated off my music, my personal life had taken that unexpected turn with the news of my first child being on its way. No question about it, I had plenty to think about, and not much time to do the thinking in.

But at the end of every day, when I was too tired to take off my clothes to get under the covers, as soon as my head hit the pillow, my eyes would open wide and I'd lie there, with no place to go but deep into my worst fears.

It's at times like that when a man needs his friends and family around him, and my crew came through in every way they could. Shanté did her best to take my mind off my troubles, and Mama and my brothers were always there to get me back in touch with my roots. G and Nate, Dre, and even Suge were solid behind me, but when it was all said and done, I had to carry that weight by myself.

Nobody was going to be able to stand trial for me and, sure as shit, no one was going to serve out my time if I got convicted. It was during that time that I learned to lean on God like I never had before. No matter what my lawyer said about trumped-up charges and police incompetence; no matter how much I heard the DA beating the drum on TV for making a stand against gang warfare . . . no matter what anybody said, I knew in the end, my life was in His hands. It's the Almighty that's got the power over life and death, the keys to heaven and hell, the sole right to bless and curse as He sees fit. We may *want* to believe we can shuffle the deck, work the angles, and stack the odds, but that's just human vanity showing through. We've got one thing open to us—prayer—and you better believe I did a lot of praying in those months before my trial.

I'd go so far as to say I got as good at praying as I did at rapping, and I had plenty of opportunity to do both as that summer started a slow slide into fall. Right alongside what was going down with me, the situation at Death Row was attracting a lot of the wrong kind of attention. Suge's gangsta style of executive management was making him a lot of enemies, and the artists on the label were starting to suffer a little from guilt by association. Not that it made much of an impact on the bottom line of our record sales and cash receipts. If anything, being on Death Row was a mark of genuine gangsta status that money couldn't buy. That logo on a CD was as good a guarantee for a chart-topper as you could get in the music business back then.

But behind the scenes, Suge's strong-arm tactics were starting to take a toll. People were afraid to work with the motherfucker and those that did had to do their job in an atmosphere of fear and intimidation. Sooner or later Suge's policies were going to come back to bite him in the ass, and later became sooner when Dr. Dre started moaning about his profit participation in the Death Row money machine. I don't know whether he had a legitmate beef or not. It wasn't any of my business to begin with. But I do know that Dre was of the opinion right then that there wouldn't have been a Death Row Records if it hadn't been for him, and maybe he was right. Whatever he thought he should be getting was probably what he deserved, but even if Suge *was* divvying up the cheddar fair and square, I think Dre would have found some other reason to get uppity.

Dre is genius. No question about that. For my money, he single-handedly made hip-hop what it is today—the best-selling form of music in the world. It was his skills in the studio that took a hardcore underground sound and plugged it into the mainstream culture. You can never take that away from him. But whether that made everything he touched a stone-cold masterpiece is something history is going to have to decide.

You take *Murder Was the Case,* for example. Now, I've heard it said that the reason that whole project got off the ground to begin with was because Suge wanted to keep Dre happy and make sure he didn't take his talents elsewhere. I'm not here to confirm or deny that shit, but I will say this. Putting a record producer, no matter how good he is, in charge of directing a long-form is a risk I don't know *I'd* be willing to take, if someone put it to me. In the music business they've got what they call "vanity projects," basically some off-the-wall idea they let an artist get away with just so he can indulge his fantasies of being the best at everything he does.

Let me tell you something, *nobody* is the best at everything they do, not even Dr. Dre. I never thought much of *Murder Was the Case,* at least not the way Dre and Suge put it together. First of all, I wasn't really about being part of another one of Dre's musical stables. I'd done that already with *The Chronic,* and I wasn't interested in being in the sequel. *Doggystyle* was my shot at establishing myself as a solo artist, and *Murder Was the Case* seemed to be just setting me back a step. Second up, I didn't exactly feature being on the cover of an album called *Murder Was the Case* when a charge of murder was what I was dealing with in real time. I got the feeling that Suge had taken the whole publicity angle one step too far by trying to hook my situation into another opportunity to move some product. I was the hottest property on the Death Row roster and to put me on the cover of an album under the words *In Beloved Memory Calvin Broadus 1971–1994* was a little bit too close for comfort, if you know what I mean.

But, having said all that, I've got to admit that the whole thing turned out a lot better than I expected. The eighteen minutes that Dre directed for the long-form video really held up despite the fact that I'm not sure he knew the difference between a camera and a catering truck. Second, the music was some of Dre's best and made everybody sound good, whether you'd been in the game awhile like me and Ice Cube, or were just then trying to get your name out there, like Sam Sneed, Clip Capone, and all the other niggers on that soundtrack that no one heard of before or since.

But, most important of all, *Murder Was the Case* kept my name out there at a time when I was fighting for my life and didn't have the focus or concentration to start working right away on a follow-up to *Doggystyle*. And maybe, in the end, that was the whole reason they pushed it out to begin with. Without Snoop Dogg, Death Row was just another record label with a fast-talking CEO and a roster of unproven talent. I put the label on the map, pure and simple, and it was in their interest, just like it was in mine, to keep my profile high.

And it worked. *Murder Was the Case* reached number one on the *Billboard* charts when it was released, and I'm guessing that at least part of the reason was that my fans thought I was making some kind of musical comment on the trial.

That was the last thing on my mind. Rappers can rhyme all they want about what's going down in the system, but if you're caught up in that system, all you're interested in is getting your ass out of harm's way. I wasn't making some bold stand for truth and justice. I wasn't pleading my case in the court of public opinion. I wasn't a symbol for all the oppression and prejudice that runs rampant in America. I was a nigger facing down a life sentence, and it's damn hard to think of a rhyme to describe *that*.

When I look back, I sometimes wonder how it is I got through those times at all. It wasn't like back in the day when they could throw me in jail and I'd come out six months later to find that nothing much had really changed. I suddenly had a lot to lose, and a lot of reasons for wanting to stay free. The fear and the tension of not knowing how much longer I could hold on to what I'd gotten was more than one man should have to endure.

But it wasn't just one man. When I go back to that time, I remember someone whose friendship and love, courage and commitment, was like a gift from God to keep me going. When I walked through the valley of the shadow of death, there was someone at my side.

His name was Tupac.

My beautiful Shanté on
our wedding day.

chapter twenty-three

loser than a brother." That's what I'd say when people asked me to talk about my feelings toward 'Pac after he'd been murdered. I meant no disrespect to my real brothers, or to my L.B. homies like G who treated me like family. But sometimes, if you're lucky, someone comes into your life who'll take up a place in your heart that no one else can fill, someone who's tighter than a twin, more with you than your own shadow, who gets deeper under your skin than your own blood and bones. That was Tupac. Know what I mean?

The brother was powerful, strong in soul and in body, with a mind that divided truth from lies like a bolt of lightning splits a tree and a spirit that put the truth he found to the test every day of his life. He lived like he rapped, full of righteous anger and always on a quest for peace. There was no other like him and there never will be again. So says Snoop Dogg, who was down with the nigger all the way.

When you live in the ghetto you hear a lot of hype about how this 'hood is better than that 'hood, or how a crew from one side of town can cut another crew from somewhere else. This city is supposed to be the bomb and that city isn't worth shit; my mama is better than your mama; my dick is bigger than your dick.

Speaking personally, I get sick of hearing it, the way we've always got to compare everything to everything else, making one thing good by making something else not as good. It's all about ranking, like nothing has any meaning unless we can measure it on a scale of one to ten, then give it a price based on the score. Word: some things just *are*, without any bad, better, best, and what they're worth can't be measured out and sold by the inch or the ounce.

Check it out: Snoop Dogg and Tupac Shakur came from two different cities on opposite coasts—L.A. and New York. We had different experiences coming up and different ways of dealing with the good and bad that shaped our lives. One was tall and, well, let's just say one wasn't so tall. One had rows, the other was cue-balled. One talked West Coast style, the other . . . well, you get the idea. What I'm trying to say is, if you use that yardstick we're all the time holding up to each other, you could find plenty of reasons why 'Pac and I should never have hung together. You could have made a case about how we were rivals, not homeboys, and how the competition between us would never allow for a friendship to grow, not to speak of a brotherhood being born.

But it just isn't true. When it all came down, none of that mattered. Long Beach or The Bronx . . . under the name, it's all the same. What counts is what brings us together, not what takes us apart.

You could say the life Tupac led was a straight 180 from mine, but I've always tended to look at what we had in common, how our histories tracked the same path, and when you come at it from that angle, the differences start to fade. We were both ghetto youngsters from broken homes, both had good grades in school but also a troublemaking streak that kept us from realizing our full potential in the classroom. He and I had that same early drive to express ourselves, me through rap and him, at first, anyway, through acting. Lots of gaffles with the cops, a second chance to try again, fame and fortune at an early age—in some ways it was like we were playing out the same script, only from different sides of the nation. It was inevitable that sooner or later our paths would cross.

But it was no sure thing that we would become homies so tight it was a legend in the rap world. To me, that friendship was one of the best things that happened during the whole reign of gangsta rap. 'Pac and I proved, once and for all, that it didn't matter where you came from and what 'hood you pledged allegiance to. There were roots that ran even deeper than your place of origin, roots that reached across the country and united us all.

Of course, it didn't hurt that the nigger had skills. His style of rap was as different from mine as it could be, but I knew from jump that he was right up there with the best of the best. After all, it takes one to know one . . . Back when I was still trying to get my game together, he was coming up with bomb albums like *2Pacalypse Now* and *Strictly 4 My N.I.G.G.A.Z.* Those were required listening for me, not because I necessarily wanted to follow his style or pick up on his approach, but because I respected the truth he was telling, like a powerful force behind his words that could make the short hairs on the back of your neck stand straight up.

But it wasn't just the music that built that bridge between us. Remember I was talking about that troublemaking streak? Probably three quarters of the niggers in America today can relate to crossing over the legal line at one time or another, but for 'Pac and me, stepping over that line was our way of proving to anybody listening that we lived by our own laws. He matched me bust for bust as a youngster, and even when he got better known, it was like he just couldn't stay out of the way of the powers that be. I remember hearing about him beating up some uppity limo driver, taking a baseball bat to a rival rapper, and punching out some Hollywood director and thinking to myself, "What is wrong with this nigger?"

But I knew all along what was wrong with him. It was the same thing wrong with me. We both had the brains and the balls to move up and make ourselves known and when you do that, you automatically become a target to the authorities.

For all that, though, 'Pac and I loved to party as much as any other motherfuckers on the block, and when you're the two dopest brothers on the nationwide scene, you better believe you get opportunities presented to you. My man could also match me blunt for blunt, bottle for bottle . . . and bitch for bitch, and we never missed a chance to strut our stuff in the finest threads cheddar could buy, making the scene in the Big Apple and out along the Sunset Strip, turning heads and taking no prisoners, pussy-wise. Did you check us out at the MTV awards back in '96, a few days before he checked out? You couldn't miss us, the come-correct players flashing signs and wearing enough gold to put Fort Knox out of business. Shit, it's no wonder Snoop and Tupac were the toast of the town, in no matter what town we were found.

But there was a place where our paths divided, a road I couldn't follow 'Pac down, even if I'd wanted to. I've seen it before—ghetto niggers walking around with a hex on them, like they were born under a bad sign, and when you see them coming down the street you're always a little surprised that they're still standing and breathing and talking like they don't even know they're living on borrowed time.

I'm not a big believer in that voodoo shit, all that John the Conquerer and mojo hand doesn't cut it with me, but when you look at a brother like 'Pac—so talented, so full of life, so ready to rule—you've got to wonder what it is that draws death to someone like that. It's almost like he was carrying around an equal measure of good and evil and sooner or later he was going to use up one and draw down hard on the other. 'Pac just ran out of the good before he got to bottom of the evil. He was fated to die young—I believe that. But knowing that doesn't make it any easier. I miss the nigger and wish he was here today to flash me that big wide smile with that front grille of white teeth shining like a row of diamonds on a pimp's ring.

By the time I started running hard with 'Pac, you could almost see in his face the knowledge he had that death was closing in. A kind of haunted look would come up in his eyes when he thought no one else was looking, a sadness that didn't have a name and was gone as soon as someone called him back into the here and now. "I will die before my time because I already feel the shadow's depth," he wrote in a poem to his friends way back in '92. "So much I wanted to accomplish before I reached my death."

But even knowing that, even knowing that Tupac Shakur's time was measured out in days and hours before he ever set foot on this planet, I can't shake the feeling that his death was a waste and that he got sacrificed in a war that never should have been fought for a prize that nobody needed to win. Ask me and I'll tell you—East Coast, West Coast; Death Row and Bad Boy; Biggie Smalls and Suge Knight—most of what you hear about all those rivalries is shit the media makes up and splashes all over their newspapers and their time slots and their glossy magazine covers to make more money.

They can turn something like a few ghetto gangsters shooting off their mouth into the crime of the century, get everyone hyped up and expecting blood and bullets in the streets of America and then, when it actually happens, they can sit back all smug and satisfied and say they told us so. Word: the media plays us all for suckers, telling stories they want us to hear and feeding us lies to keep us coming back.

Is there an East Coast–West Coast gangsta war? What do you think? You got niggers with red bandannas and niggers with blue bandannas killing each other for no other reason than their fashion code. Why shouldn't you have Harlem niggers killing Compton niggers over who's got the dopest rap stars on their team? It's like I said, some fool has always got to be the best, and the fool that isn't won't stop until he is. But when you take that natural competitive streak and make it into a national scandal, talking about who dissed who and who's selling more records and who's got the biggest bottom line, then someone's got to take responsibility for that bullshit sooner or later. And when people start offing each other just to prove something in front of the millions of gawkers that are watching the gangsta soap opera unfold every day on the evening news, then we got to stop playing the game by the rules they're laying down.

People ask me all the time about how Tupac got himself killed. Was it Biggie and Puffy and André, just like Tupac said it was, that ambushed him outside that studio in Times Square? Was Stretch Walker killed execution style as a payback for the job? Who killed the Notorious B.I.G.? Was Suge behind the death of Orlando Anderson like all the ugly rumors had it?

I answer all those questions with one of my own: are you fucking crazy? You think, even if I knew the story behind all that death and destruction, that I would go tell any fool who wanted his ears tickled with the latest gangsta gossip? You think I want to perp that shit for one hour longer or one corpse more than it's already gone on? I could tell you stories that would make your blood run cold, and those are exactly the same stories I'm going to take with me to my own grave. Remember what I told you at the very beginning of this book. Snoop Dogg is about increasing the peace, not giving motherfuckers another reason to even some score that never should have been kept in the first place. Brothers and sisters, listen to me. We've got to stop killing each other. We've got to turn our rage and our righteous anger on the target where it belongs—the system that keeps us oppressed and down and addicted to crack and attacking in the dead of night like wild animals tearing at each other's throats.

Have I got something to hide? You're damn straight. It's called my ass, and I'm going to keep it out of the line of fire for as long as I can. I made myself a promise when 'Pac died: I'm going to be part of the solution, not the problem. The problem is, niggers don't know how to live together in harmony. The solution is, we've got to educate and elevate. We've got to spread the peace. Before it's too late.

The way I see it, 'Pac didn't understand that. He didn't have clarity on the issue, not until the very end, and by that time, he had to reap what he'd sown. He got up in people's faces because that's how he got taught in the ghetto—you stake out your turf and you defend it to the death. Which is exactly what happened. Hell, he even got me involved for a while there, back in '96 when we did "2 of Americaz Most Wanted," with the video that showed Biggie and Puffy getting payback for setting up 'Pac. I did it because he asked me to and because he was my friend, but I'll tell you this for free. It didn't help the situation, and it took 'Pac's dying for me to understand that I could either help or hurt and the choice was up to me.

A lot of things changed when Tupac died. And not just for me. I think a lot of brothers in the music business woke up to the fact that the job we had was about more than just selling units and filling concert halls. We were role models, and we had to walk a fine line between telling the truth about what was really going down on the streets and offering some kind of hope that maybe, one day, we could make it better. Fighting among ourselves, gunning each other down, and talking trash just because we came from different 'hoods or cut on different labels wasn't going to make anything better. It wasn't enough just to tell it like it is anymore. It was time to tell it like it could be.

'Pac never had a chance to do that, but I know he was heading that way. In an interview he gave out on Rikers Island after he was sent up on that bullshit sex-abuse charge, he told his fans his "thug life" was over, that it was time to put something positive back into the community, and that the change was going to start with him.

I believe it would have, if he'd only had the chance.

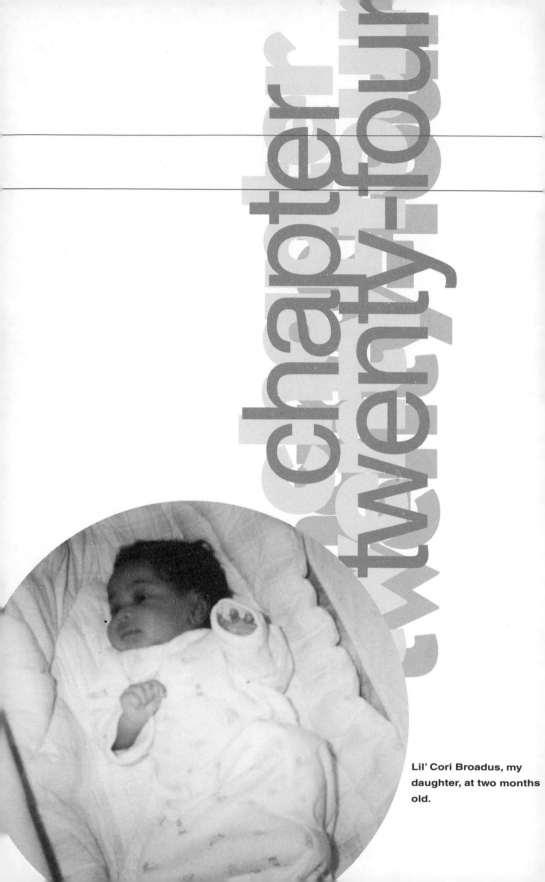

chapter twenty-four

Lil' Cori Broadus, my
daughter, at two months
old.

chapter twenty-four

ase number BAO86649, *Calvin Broadus (a.k.a. Snoop Doggy Dogg)* v. *The People of the State of California,* finally got itself going November 27, 1995, in department 110, room #9-302 of the Los Angeles Criminal Courts Building. It was going on three years after the fucking fact.

Three years is a long time to live with a possible life sentence hanging over your head, and I'd be stretching the truth if I told you I ever really got used to it. There wasn't a day that passed during that long wait when I didn't think about what was waiting for me at the far side of that moment when the jury handed down their verdict. It was like living with a secret that was too big to hide and too personal to tell. You just had to carry it by yourself, the last thing you think about before you go to sleep and the first thing you think about in the A.M.

But there's another way of looking at it, too. Knowing that all the good things that had come to me could be geese at any moment taught me to appreciate those blessings all the more. I wasn't looking for what was due me, or regretting what I'd passed by—I was tuned into what was happening right then and there, and if, for some reason, the scenario wasn't cool, well, I knew it could get a lot worse.

And life has a habit of rolling on, with or without your ass following along. I had a lot of things to be thankful for during that time. First and foremost was the birth of my son Cordé, back in '94. Looking down at a brand new homeboy, sitting tight in his mama's arms, gave me a whole other perspective on what was real, down deep, and what was just a waste of time. I had somebody else that depended on me now, not just the niggers on my payroll or the 'bloods that hung around for the free chronic and malt liquor and take-out chicken they could charge to my American Express platinum card. Those motherfuckers could take care of themselves if they had to, but Cordé—he was totally and 100 percent in need of a father, and from the first time I picked up him up from Shanté and held his little body, about as light as an elbow, I was totally and 100 percent down for the job. No matter what else I did with myself, I knew nothing was more important than giving my son everything he needed to feel safe and free and fine about himself. You're always hearing people talk about wanting to leave a legacy. Well, I got news for you fools—raise your kids up right. That's the best legacy you can ever bestow on the world.

With my new son and his mother, I made the move to the West Valley, out toward Calabasas, which is about as far from Long Beach Boulevard as you can get and still hear English spoken. They had trees and lawns and wide, winding streets where people walked their dogs night and day, and there wasn't any G'd-up bawla's driving gangsta lean, looking for someone to pop a cap on. The fact was, there weren't a whole lot of black folks to be seen anywhere around, and the looks I got driving my SUV with my son kicking it in his top-of-the-line baby seat next to me was a whole other kind of intimidation. But I didn't mind. As long as I had the cash, they could kiss my ass. I was there to stay.

But not if the cops and the D.A.'s office had anything to say about it. In case I ever had a minute to forget that they were breathing down my neck, they made sure to remind me, like almost a year later, when they filed additional charges against me for conspiracy and being an accessory after the fact. I never did quite put it together how I could have been part of the crime before, during, and after it took place, but it seems like that was what they were going for, and nothing was going to stop them until they'd hammered me to the wall with a nail gun.

All three of us standing trial—me, Malik, and Sean Dogg—had our own lawyers, and the one that had gotten hold of Sean's case was none other than Johnnie Cochran, Jr., who, of course, would go on to spring O. J. Simpson in the so-called trial of the century. From where I was sitting, Johnnie was a little too flashy for his own good, and as the case got under way, I was glad he wasn't the one representing me. It was like the motherfucker was more interested in polishing his own reputation than covering his client's ass, at least that's the way I saw it. When it comes to the law, I prefer my lawyers to stay close to the ground and do their homework. Don't be grandstanding while my life is at stake.

I've got to hand it to Cochran, through. For all his hype talk and $5,000 suits, he really took care of business for Sean and had the charges dropped before we even got into the courtroom. Now it was just down to me and Malik.

The prosecution team, which was being headed up by a deputy D.A. named Ed Nison and included a brother named Bobby Grace, came on strong from jump. It was obvious to all of us that Nison thought he had an airtight conviction going in, and his only job was to huff and puff and blow down the house of cards we had built up for a case of self-defense. He laid it on thick, talking about all the "pursuit, pressure, and posturing" we had done that ended with the icing of Woldemariam, who, I found out, went by the name Little Smooth in the By Yerself Hustlers. The story, as he laid it out, was that, after the first gaffle out in front of my place, me, Malik, and Sean had gone looking for the motherfucker and, when we found him, shot him in the back as he was trying to run away. Nison even put up a big autopsy photo of Little Smooth to get his point across. "A picture is worth a thousand words," he said, and it wouldn't be the only time, in the days to come, that the thought crossed my mind that this cracker would make a good rapper if he'd just loosen up and let it flow a little freer.

Kenner, who was representing me on Death Row's dime, and another lawyer named Donald Re, who'd also been paid by Suge to pick up Malik's case, played it straight, retelling the truth as we had laid it down to them and promising to prove to the jury that it was all about self-defense, open and shut. But they didn't stop at making promises. The fact was, with all the gang-related hysteria that the media was whipping up, and the controversy about my music that was only adding fuel to the flame, we had what you might call the burden of proof to convince the jury that even gangstas have a right to defend themselves.

And that meant we had to start pounding away at the prosecution's version of the story before it had a chance to get settled in the jurors' minds. Lucky for us, they handed over all the ammunition we needed. It seems that Woldemariam's two By Yerself homies had gotten the bright idea after the shooting to hide the piece he'd been carrying to make it look like we'd opened fire on an unarmed man. Both of the niggers, London and Joseph, later took back their lies, which tended to what you might call *undercut their credibility* as reliable witnesses. Re and Kenner drove the point home by showing how the cops had taken the two at their word and, based on their accounts, had decided to charge us with a first-degree murder beef.

The next step was to prove that Little Smooth really was the mad-dog banger everyone who knew him said he was. Kenner brought out the facts that the nigger had been arrested twice for acting nuts with a gat, one time waving it around in a schoolyard and another time carrying a loaded weapon on the Blue Line train. They made it a point to explain how my moving into the Palms apartment was like I was stepping directly into Woldemariam's turf, and that, by the rules of the street, was a challenge that couldn't go unanswered.

All props to Kenner and Re, who knew their shit and came to court every day with their eyes sharp on the target, but, even so, by the end of the first week, it wouldn't have taken any legal eagle to start punching holes in the prosecution's case. It's one thing to build up a story based on flimsy, circumstantial evidence, but when that story starts coming apart at the seams because your witnesses can't keep their testimony straight, then you've got to wonder whether you should be in another line of work.

For instance, the prosecution brought up this little twelve-year-old Eagle Scout who claimed he saw Malik driving by with a "menacing look" on his face just before the killing. Now, Malik is a pretty menacing-looking nigger at the best of times, which that definitely wasn't. But it didn't take much cross-examination for that youngster to fold, by getting him to admit he'd been more than one hundred yards away at the time. Same with the next witness, who testified that he also saw Malik on the prowl in an alley in back of his apartment, before it came out that the brother he was talking about was lighter skinned than my bodyguard.

But it was their third call of the day that really wreaked havoc. This 'blood also claimed he had seen Malik looking for Little Smooth and that he'd also witnessed the whole shoot-out go down. It was only on the stand that our team forced it out of him that he was high on indo at the time and wasn't even wearing the specs he needed to see his hand in front of his face. Finally, as he watched his whole fairy tale crumble in front of him, the prosecution's star witness admitted that he'd lied to the cops when he said he'd seen Malik pull the trigger.

In his courthouse steps interview at the end of what must have been one of the downest days of his career, Nison tried to bluff his way out. "Every gang case I have put on," he told reporters, "someone will get up and say, 'I lied to the police.' It's very typical in the situation."

That might have been, but none of those reporters asked the question I wanted asked: "Why the hell would you put on someone who gets up and says they lied to you in the first place?"

By the time we were into week two of the trial, the People's case was starting to look like a rag doll getting chewed apart by a pit bull. When London got to the stand, he admitted what everyone connected with the case already knew: he and Dushaun Joseph had lifted the gat out of Little Smooth's waistband to make it look like he was just an innocent victim of a vicious gangsta rapper and his cutthroat crew. But he didn't stop there. Woldemariam had a reputation on the street as being a hothead—the way London put it, when things got a little rough for Little Smooth "he didn't think rationally."

Right about then, Kenner went for the jugular. Why, he asked, had London lied about his homey carrying a gun?

"At the time, the only thing I was thinking about was my friend," he answered.

Kenner pressed in. "You didn't say anything about the gun because you wanted to frame Mr. Lee and Mr. Broadus. Correct?"

London shook his head and muttered "No," but it was too late. Chalk one up for our side: now that London had a motive for hiding the gun, anything else he might testify to would be suspect. And Kenner wasn't about to hold off now. For what must have been an hour he grilled that poor nigger about the tussle outside my place until London had to admit that he never saw me squaring off against anyone.

"Is it your testimony that you never saw Snoop do anything?" was Kenner's last question to the witness.

"Correct," London answered, so low you could hardly hear him.

From almost the very beginning, it seemed like the facts of the case, and the way they were being presented, were going our way. I began hoping against hope that I wasn't just bullshitting myself and that I really did have reason to feel like I might one day be able to put this all behind me and walk away a free man. It was almost too much to believe, after so long a time hauling that fear behind me like a ball and chain, and I tried to read the faces of the jurors to see if I could get a clue there about what they might be feeling and thinking.

Ever try to look at a face and imagine what the person is really thinking? Those poor citizens had been sitting in that box day after day for going on five weeks now and all I could see was what looked like boredom mixed with a little daydreaming and wishful thinking—like they were wishing we'd all just forget the whole thing and go home. The further down the road of justice we got, the less anyone seemed to care about a bunch of niggers swearing and scuffling and shooting at each other. I got the feeling those jurors would have just as soon let us kill each other off as to have to listen to the low-down dealings of some fool gangstas trying to prove how hardcore they were. I didn't know how they were feeling about Little Smooth, but I sometimes thought they were going to run my ass into the joint just to make someone pay for all that wasted time.

But I was wrong. No matter how bored or disgusted those folks might have looked to me, they were up there taking care of business, listening and thinking and filing away the facts and doing the best they could to decide what was real and what was right and what had really happened and why. It wasn't an easy job, but they did it because they knew it was important, and that if they were sitting where me and Malik were sitting, they'd want someone to take it seriously, too. I'll always be grateful to them for that, no matter how things might have turned out.

It was a couple of days before Christmas when the case took a whole new turn and the crossfire got real thick, real fast. The prosecution played their strongest hand, claiming that Woldemariam couldn't have opened fire first because the forensics proved that he'd been shot in the back. Now, if they could have made that stick, everything else that came before would have been washed down the drain. Nobody is going to stand up for any motherfucker who shoots someone in the back, and it was a do-or-die situation for us to prove that Little Smooth had been facing the right direction to see what was about to come down on him.

The whole case hinged on where, over his body, those slugs had made their mark. The DA's office called an L.A. County medical examiner, who testified that the wounds had been in his back. In cross-examination, Kenner, Re, and another member of the team, Marsha Morrison, lit into this poor fool like attack dogs. Before it was over they got him to admit that he had written in his autopsy report that the wounds were in the "lateral" portion of the body and that in "common, everyday language," "lateral" means "the side."

The way we were laying it out was that Woldemariam had been spun around by the force of the hit and that the bullets had traveled across his body, from side to side, and not through it, back to front. There was even another case, a while earlier, where the cops had shot and killed a woman and claimed that the force of the bullets had turned her around in the same way so that it just looked like she'd been hit running away. The chief of police at that time, Willie Williams, had made a statement to that effect, and Kenner and the others kept threatening to haul his ass into the chair as an expert witness.

But there was no need. By the time we got through the medical testimony, everyone on our side had the feeling that we stood a better than average chance of walking away from this thing. Aside from all the fucked-up testimony that the prosecution had brought forward, there was also the fact that the cops had lost Little Smooth's clothes, along with some bullet casings and other vital evidence, somewhere between the crime scene and the lab. It just showed a pattern of police incompetence and a rush to justice that would echo even louder a year later when O.J. got his day in court.

The more we looked at what had gone down in the past five weeks, the more sense it made to just let the case speak for itself. Kenner and the others decided on a bold move. On the last day of January 1996, we opened our case by calling our first witness, a mechanic named John Mojica, who worked in an auto-body shop and testified he saw a black man with a gun get out of a Chevy Blazer and walk down the alley behind his shop the day of the murder. A Blazer. Not a Cherokee. The motherfucker was a mechanic. He should know the difference.

And that was that. One witness up. One witness down. Originally, we'd had fifteen lined up, but the truth was, the only part of the prosecution's story that seemed worth arguing about was the claim that Malik had been prowling around in my Jeep looking for his victim. Someone else was obviously out there that day. It could have easily been a case of mistaken identity. Other than that, we'd already made our defense by tearing apart the case against us. The defense rested.

On February 14, 1996, the case was turned over to the jury. Six days later they came back with the verdict. Innocent.

The word sounded loud and clear as I sat at the defense table, my eyes closed and my hands folded in prayer.

I was free . . . free at last.

My youngbloods—
Little Snoop Dogg,
Big Spank Dogg,
and sister Cori.

chapter twenty-five

Sometimes when you're putting down a rap you get stuck on a word. You're trying to find a rhyme, but it's more than that. The word you're looking for has got to pull together everything you're trying to say in the flow without breaking the rhythm, and, at the same time, it's got to be clear enough that everyone knows exactly what you're busting.

Sometimes you find that word and sometimes you don't. But sometimes something else entirely happens and you find *another* word, one that comes out of left field, and while it doesn't exactly fit what you were looking for, it sends the rap off into a whole other spin, something doper and deeper and more surprising that you could have expected. And what you end up with is an entirely new thing, better than what you were thinking of to begin with, and all because that one word came into your skull and turned everything upside down.

Well, rapping is like life, if you know what I mean. You got a flow going, you think it's going to keep up like that until the final fade, so you've got every move mapped out before it happens. Then, one little thing happens, like a word you can't quite fit into the rhyme, and the whole thing does a 180 and you're back where you started, trying to stay one step ahead of the next curve.

For me, that one word was *innocent.* The moment that jury foreman spoke it out, nothing in my life was ever the same again. Now, maybe that sounds a little off to you. After all, a nigger spends three years with his ass on hold, then gets off the hook and is free to walk out of the courtroom and get back to what he was doing before all the shit went down in the first place.

But it wasn't like that for me. I couldn't go back. There was nothing there for me. The only direction I could move in was forward, toward a future that was full of unknowns, where the only thing you could depend on was the grace and mercy of God. The life I'd lived up to that point was over and done with. Whatever else was waiting for me on the far side of tomorrow, one thing was for sure—it was going to be different from what came before.

The night after the acquittal, I threw a monster party at a steak house called Monty's not far from my new place. Everyone was there, from my Death Row homies to the legal team, from my family and Tupac to anyone else that meant anything to me in the world. It was a time for celebration, a time to rejoice, and everybody was getting into the spirit.

But there was a moment that night that I'll never forget, sitting at the head of this big table, piled high with fine food and the best liquor, with old friends and new on either side of me, passing blunts and laughing and grooving to the hip-hop that was playing full bore out the PA.

It was like, all of a sudden, the whole room went quiet inside my head and as I looked from face to face down along that table, I heard myself thinking, as clear as if I was alone in an empty room, *This is it. The way it is now. What was, is over. What will be, is beginning. Thank you, God, for bringing me this far. And thank you, God, for taking me the rest of the way.*

I'd been a Long Beach Crip, a con, a drug dealer, and a gangbanger. I'd made my way up the ladder to the pinnacle of superstardom. I'd almost lost it all and got it all back in the nick of time. I would never forget where I'd come from and never lose touch with the roots that went deep, back to those places and faces and times I've been describing in this book. But what else was true was that I wasn't going back. I couldn't. I'd seen too much, been through too much, to ever be satisfied being the person I was before I heard the word that delivered me from a living death.

So I sat there and smiled and took everyone's congratulations, my homies' high fives and the kisses of the bitches, and the whole time it was like there was this silent place inside my head where I was totally on my own, asking the same question over and over: "Who am I now?"

It was up to me to find the answer, and over the next couple of years I studied hard on it. My rap career continued to climb, and I kept at it, grateful to have a way to express myself, even while the circumstances and situations around me went through some hardcore changes. The Death Row story is one you can read in the headlines—how Dre left the label and Suge kept pushing his luck until he ran up against the limits of his own pride and ambition and gangsta methodology.

My second solo album, *Tha Doggfather,* came out in '96 and was almost as big a smash as *Doggystyle,* even without Dre behind the board. The fact is, I started stepping up to producing myself and, with the help of some old homies like G and Daz, we put together one motherfucker of a tune stack. I still had the magic and it was as potent as ever.

Don't get me wrong. I was thankful every time a copy of *Tha Doggfather* sold, just like I was thankful every time someone slipped it in their player to give it a spin. When people support me and my music I consider that an act of friendship, like you're all saying you believe in me and want me to keep on keeping on. But the truth is, it's the keeping on part that was taking up my attention at the time—just like it still does today. Like I said, I'd been through too much to go back. The only direction left was forward, and anyone who tells you they can predict what's going to happen to you next year, next month, or tomorrow, is lying through their teeth. So I had to take it on faith . . . God had a plan for my life and it was up to me now to play the game by His rules.

And that meant taking care of first things first. It wasn't too long before I was cleared of murder charges that Shanté broke the news that she was pregnant again, and I didn't waste any time after being acquitted in asking her to marry me. It was something I should have done a long time before and just one more thing that hearing that word *innocent* had done to put my priorities in order.

Innocent. There's probably no one out there reading this book that can lay claim to that word—at least, not totally.

I didn't go looking to kill Philip "Little Smooth" Woldemariam, but that doesn't mean I didn't have something to do with his dying. We both lived in a violent world, and we both did our part to perpetuate that violence. Both of us lived by the sword and one of us died by it. It's up to the other one to walk away from that fate and create a different scenario for himself and his family. Marrying Shanté was the first step in that direction.

But when my second son, Cordell—who we call "Little Snoop" because of his resemblance to his old man—was born, I was one more time reminded that, if there *is* such a thing as innocence in this world, it's in the face of a little baby. Looking down at my son, like I'd look down on Cori, my daughter, born two years later, I wondered if that wasn't a way for those of us who'd lost our innocence in this world to get back at least a part of it—by protecting and caring and looking out for the youngsters, the ones that still have a chance to do it all better than we did, and hang on to a little bit more of that trust and openness and joy of living that every kid brings with him into this cold, hard world. I had it once, but I lost it along the way. My kids have it now, and I'll do what I can to help them hold on to it as long as they can.

Being a family man and getting right with responsibility was the most important step I took in trying to lay claim to some small part of that word *innocent* that set me free. The next step was to try and build on what was positive in my music and cut loose the negative that had been sticking to my sound and my name from the shit that went down at Death Row. The reality is, I never was part of Suge's gangsta style of doing business, but that was a claim I could never back up as long as I was part of his scene. Like so much else in my life, it was time to make a clean break and a fresh start.

It all came clear to me in March of '97 with the news of the drive-by shooting of Biggie Smalls. Whoever did the job, and for whatever reason, didn't matter anymore. The fact was, too many niggers were dying trying to live up to some bullshit outlaw code that had nothing to do about getting on with the business at hand: making this world a better place to live . . . for everyone.

It's like Tupac said: the thug life was over. It was time to find a new way of expressing ourselves, a creative channel for our anger and a different perspective on getting what was due us. Gangsta rap and the lifestyle that went with it had shaken a lot of fools awake. But now that we had gotten everyone's attention, we had to offer something else to move the game to the next round. For me, that next move was leaving Death Row Records and cutting my ties with what it had come to represent.

I've got to hand it to Suge. I believe he knew it was right for me to make that move, and while he wasn't a fool about it and made sure he got a good return on his investment, in the end he let me go, in peace and blessing. Suge may have a lot to answer for from the niggers he undercut, overpowered, and generally fucked around in one way or the other—but as far as Snoop Dogg is concerned, the slate is clean.

My choice to leave Death Row had a lot to do with the destination I had in mind: No Limit Records, where a stone-cold genius on the order of Dr. Dre had set up shop. Master P is just one of those motherfuckers who's got the goods and can deliver, every time out. If anyone is going to take hip-hop into the twenty-first century, it's going to be him, and if you need evidence, I suggest you listen to my two No Limit albums, *Da Game Is to Be Sold, Not to Be Told* and *No Limit Top Dogg*. That's the sound of the future, here today.

Working with No Limit has given me the kind of freedom I always looked for in making my music. Master P is on hand to give me guidance and suggestions, but there's no one looking over my shoulder trying to direct the flow one way or the other, and as a result, I can open it up and make room for both new sounds and old homies. It was my particular pleasure, for instance, to get Dre and Warren G and Nate Dogg back on my crew for *Top Dogg*, and from jump the idea was to take the best of what was happening right in the moment and mix it up with the best of what we all had laid down coming up to that point. That's the way the best shit always happens—building on what comes before and reaching out for what is just about to come.

There's another piece to the No Limit equation that adds up for me. Being based in Baton Rouge, Louisiana, feels like coming full circle, back to the Deep South where my people were from to start with. I keep for my family a place out there for when I'm doing business, and there's something about the slowed-down and mellow pace of Southern life that soothes my soul like nowhere else. No Limit feels like home, and these days, home is where I most like to spend my time.

So, I keep on keeping on. My family comes first; rap is what I do and my homeboys are always there to remind me where I came from. It's like working on a mix in the studio. You go heavy on the bass, then back off a bit. You add a little echo, then take it out. You go back to the beginning and try to listen like you're hearing it for the very first time. Then, if you're lucky, maybe at four o'clock one morning, when you're all alone in the studio and the whole world is sleeping out beyond those soundproof walls, it suddenly comes together. You get the perfect balance, when everything locks into everything else and the final result is something bigger and better than all the separate pieces by themselves. That's what I try to find these days in my life—a balance, a way to mix all the parts together so they'll harmonize.

But it's nothing I can do by myself. I've tried and my mix just doesn't cut it. These days I look to God to get me through each day, to guide me on my path and to help others along their way. He's taken me this far; I've got no reason to believe He won't be with me for the rest of the ride. This book, as much as it is about where I came from and how I got here, is really a story about what happens next. This has all been preparation. *Now* I'm ready to begin, to get busy with God's plan.

As far as I can tell, that day in court, when I heard that verdict pronounced, marked *Paid* on one whole part of the Snoop Dogg saga. I was set up to be a spokesperson for the gangsta lifestyle, a ghetto prophet, rapping for the voiceless masses. And maybe I was. But the truth is, I was never fully down with that role. It wasn't my thing to be a symbol, set up high where people could worship me or try to knock me off the pedestal. I understand that youngbloods need role models and heroes, but I have to ask myself—who died and made *me* the Great Black Hope? I'm a nigger from Long Beach, California, who's done a lot of things wrong and couple of things right.

So now, when I rap, I rap for one person—Snoop Dogg. The nigger's been through a lot and he knows a thing or two, and if you ask him, he'll tell you:

Increase the peace.

Spread the music.

Elevate and educate.

Word: it starts with you and me.